BEN HOGAN'S SHORT GAME SIMPLIFIED

Also by Ted Hunt:

Ben Hogan's Magical Device

BEN HOGAN'S SHORT GAME SIMPLIFIED

THE SECRET TO HOGAN'S GAME FROM 120 YARDS AND IN

TED HUNT

Skyhorse Publishing

Skyhorse Publishing books may be purchased in bulk at special discounts for sales promotion, corporate gifts, fund-raising, or educational purposes. Special editions can also be created to specifications. For details, contact the Special Sales Department, Skyhorse Publishing, 555 Eighth Avenue, Suite 903, New York, NY 10018 or info@skyhorsepublishing.com.

www.skyhorsepublishing.com

10 9 8 7 6 5 4 3 2 1

Library of Congress Cataloging-in-Publication Data
Hunt, Ted.
Ben Hogan's short game simplified : the secret to Hogan's game from 120 yards and in / Ted Hunt.
p. cm.
Includes bibliographical references and index.
ISBN 978-1-61608-112-6 (hardcover : alk. paper)
1. Short game (Golf) 2. Hogan, Ben, 1912-1997. I. Title.
GV979.S54H86 2010
796.352'3—dc22
2010023815

Printed in China

This book is written for people who gain pleasure from the challenge of golf, even while they struggle with the contemplation of its mysteries.

CONTENTS

Four friends with their backs to the sometimes wild Pacific Ocean and their eyes ahead to the challenge of the ninth hole at Monterey Peninsula Country Club wondering how they might squeeze some money from their opponents of the moment.

PREFACE

HOW CAN AN AMATEUR GOLFER STRIKE THE BALL PROPERLY WITHOUT THE PRACTICE REGIME OF A PROFESSIONAL?

THE GENERAL PROBLEM:

Not being a professional golf instructor, I was self-conscious about writing my first book: *Ben Hogan's Magical Device*. Sean Connery, a golfing friend, after reviewing the first rough draft said, "Mr. Hogan might be pirouetting in his grave." It is possible that the original 007 may have been right—and it is also reasonable to assume that you might ask the same question—so let me give a bit of background which helped define the problem and its answer.

PHOTO CREDIT: First Cut Golf

Ben Hogan hitting a nine iron punch shot to win his first individual tour victory at Pinehurst, North Carolina, in 1940.

Hoping to ignore the possibility of defiling one of golf's greatest icons, I tried to reassure myself that I had been a professional in football at least, playing with the BC Lions of the Canadian Football League (you might not have heard of me . . . I was second-string behind the league's leading rusher, Willie Fleming from Detroit—and Joe Kapp, the Californian who later led the Minnesota Vikings to the Super Bowl, was reluctant to throw me the ball because at the University of British Columbia we often thrashed Joe and his University of California teammates in our rugby days). My point is, I knew what professional standards were all about. Also, I had a couple of degrees in human kinetics—studying physiology, applied physics, and the laws of learning. Better still, I had a doctorate in history, so I knew how to gather information which could help determine "Hogan's Secret." There was an excess of written opinion trying to explain Hogan's ball striking capability, and the theories ranged from the extra-stiff shafts in his clubs to the way he kicked in his right knee at address. It is interesting now to hear that Tiger Woods has been analyzing Hogan's swing, and that his driver has the same specifications. There is little doubt that some touring professionals found variations on Hogan's theme by feel—Arnold Palmer and his father found their way to stop the left wrist from breaking down at impact—but there was no explanation that could allow replication by others. So I was determined to find the answer.

Please remember, the following revelations are not my golf techniques. They are Ben Hogan's techniques—as described to me, piece by piece, by fascinated professional golfers who studied Hogan, or who had at least observed him with an analytical eye. As Kafka said, "The writer has nothing to say. He just presents evidence."

On the Hogan topic, I had the privilege of interviewing Arnold Palmer, Sam Snead, Jack Nicklaus, Alvie Thompson, George Knudson, and Mike Souchak. I caddied for Moe Norman, Ted Kroll, Jay Hebert, Bing Crosby, and Babe Didrickson Zaharias. Then I was lucky enough to play with Stan Leonard, Moe Norman, Davis Love III, Dick Zokol, Jim Thorpe, Paul Azinger, Corey Pavin, Tom Kite, Ernie Brown, Brad Faxon, Jim Furyk, Joey Sindelar, and Bob Hope—all of whom had observations and stories about Ben Hogan. These experiences were fortuitous and pleasurable.

From these informed sources I gathered snippets of detailed information. Their insights were always in their own language, which was mostly slang terminology with perhaps a demonstration thrown if they had the time: "wringing the towel," "changing the chuck on the lever," "buckling the wrist," "rolling the wrist," "arch and twist," "keep a flat wrist," "square to square."

It was my job to sift through the verbiage, and to put it into understandable, and universal, anatomical terms for reliable transmission.

In the hopes of persuading you to give Hogan's short game system an honest try, I will get into the good stuff as quickly as possible . . . but you have to know that Ben Hogan is not a "quick fix" kind of guy, and the "engine room" of his golf swing—and the "secret" within it—should be put in a context to be best understood. A lot of golfers don't have the patience to give Hogan a week's work, even when they have heard that touring professionals spend months on a swing

Hogan out of the rough at Carnoustie for the British Open win in 1953.

PHOTO CREDIT: Dundee Press

change—but if you have just one week's worth of patience, you can change your game significantly.

Hogan mastered the game of golf by trial and error, so analyzing his swing is like peeling back the layers of an onion. Fortunately, you don't have to accept all of Hogan's studied moves, but please be sure to give a full effort to reading about the nucleus of his artful swing, namely: the Magical Device—which is the way he used his connected arms and shoulders; and his "secret"—which is the way he moved his lead hand. These two actions can adapt nicely to your own swing. However, you should at least know the reasons he did certain foundation things. Therefore I shall put a review of Hogan's fundamentals toward the back of the book in Chapter Eighteen so that you can refer to them, if and when necessary.

Hogan spent four arduous years in a daily regimen to find what worked in the swing and what didn't, a torturous procedure he called "digging it out of the dirt" (now a Hogan cliché). It was this process he might recommend to people he didn't like, or to those who were brash enough to sidle up and ask for his secret. Depending upon his unpredictable mood, Hogan might invite the inquirer, even though a colleague, to work it out on his own, and/or would deflect the annoyance with a misleading suggestion.

Hearing references to Hogan hitting thousands of balls per week, most amateurs might think that this is what they have to follow in order to play a decent game—fortunately, I found that this is not necessarily so. This book will tell you how to ingrain the system and then keep it "on hand" with short but specific work at home.

If you would like to master Hogan's repeating swing, here's what to do:

- Begin with Chapters Two and Three, and read how to use the Magical Device with putting and chipping—theoretically fifty-five percent of your game. And if numbers get your attention: My average putts per round went from thirty-three to twenty-seven, and my gross score bettered my age nine times in competition the first season with Hogan's system.
- Learn and ingrain Hogan's Magical Device with a simple psych-lab formula: Take thirty short putts per day from six feet, and thirty short chips per day from fifteen feet. Keep it up for one week and amaze yourself. The downside is that you will earn the jealous enmity of your friends—who probably liked

you only because you kept losing to them anyway. Hogan had something very close to this laboratory-proven method by simply advising: "Practice with the Magical Device for fifteen minutes per day for seven days, and you've got it."

This book will present ten stages of Ben Hogan's swing system in detail, and will provide the necessary related drills to secure these images within your memory bank. You will learn ways to review the details at home in just a few minutes per day. Using Hogan's short game system, physically fit amateur golfers can play the game well enough to maintain a single-digit handicap and make their presence known in club competitions.

And for that ambition, wouldn't it be valuable to be able to call on "Hogan's System" with nothing more than two or three practice swings? To be able to hurry from an unexpected meeting, late to the first tee, and actually be confident about playing well because you have a system to tune in? To not have to worry about the first putt on the first green, even without a warm-up putt, because you know exactly what to do? You have a structured system—and by God it works.

After talking to hundreds of club players, it has become clear that what amateur golfers most want—and/or need—is a thorough and descriptive instruction on the part of golf which impacts them to the greatest degree, that is, the short game from 120 yards and in. The focus on this part of the game amounts to approximately eighty percent of the amateur golfers' actions, and happily, it is the short game which holds the most realistic chance of improvement through a study of Hogan's short game system. It is a plain fact that part-time golfers need a source for reminders because they are not at the course every day.

Golfers in small clinics have shown solid growth when Ben Hogan's system is introduced—first through putting and chipping—and accompanied by detailed pictorial demonstrations in a series of poses which they can review, contemplate, and practice for themselves in front of a mirror. There are also assigned drills for short daily practices for the one-week initiation period. The instruction in this book will be divided into sections based upon ten stages of Hogan's swing. One at a time, these sections will present a focus upon the basic posture to be examined, then to be followed by key details which accompany the main move.

It has become apparent to me, that if amateur golfers examine the first stage of the Hogan system through the simple act of putting—and are reminded that the rejuvenated Phil Mickelson has changed to the same technique—the next steps from the flag out to the 120 yard marker are more easily understood, and as a result, more easily done. There is the realization that by focusing on Hogan's position of the torso and hands at impact—and how they got there—a simple putt is the impact zone for full swing, in miniature. This valuable image of the action for the clubface and hands at impact is stored for use when visualization is needed prior to a full shot. This mental review is so useful because a feel for the impact zone is always the key to good shot-making.

Unfortunately for most golfers, the bad habits used while putting, such as poor posture combined with incorrect and active use of the hands, come back to haunt them on the course—especially around the green. Hogan's system is designed so that the hand position through impact for the putt is the same as the hand position for impact with the drive—and every bit as stable.

It has also become clear that a great majority of amateur golfers have never been taught golf as a system but have "picked up" the game in unrelated pieces—usually starting as an arm swing with the driver, because this is the club used for the opening of play, and has the most dramatic action. Of course speaking practically, the driver remains the most dangerous club to use. Most golfers "learned" by watching television, or listening to friends for Band-Aid tips at their club . . . with miracle ideas from magazines thrown in. None of these sources of information provide the full picture of the golf swing in a context, so that this incomplete structure is not, by definition, a system which can guide the golfer when in action out on the course.

As a result, the general problem remains: Most golfers do not understand the structure required for success within the three fundamental swing systems—and they do not know which one will give them the best chance for a strong and repeating swing into the ball.

Let us agree for the moment that the power for impact in a golf swing comes from three basic sources:

- The arm swing—where power for the hit is dominated by hands and arms. This system may well suit muscled and athletic young men for a while—until they want more control over where that lashed ball is heading. The arm swing, however, is not a useful servant for the average middle-aged golfer—although admittedly, it is the easiest swing with which to make a start in this complex game. A reliance on the hand action almost guarantees golf shots with poor direction consistency (as in army golf—left rough, right rough, left . . .) because the changing hand movement changes the angle of the clubface as well. Further, the demands and pressures of career and family severely limit the amount of time that can be devoted to hitting balls, weight-training, and preparing for competition. And as the body changes from the high levels of shoulder and arm strength and the flexibility enjoyed during undergraduate years of college . . . the weekend warrior watches his/her game sink slowly into the handicap bog known as "double digit." Mercifully, there is a way to earn a single-digit level—follow Hogan.

- Leg drive is another source of power for the long, strong shot. The legs, however, eventually betray all once "light foot" lads and lasses. The early Scots, with energetic pronation and supination, lashed the ball into offshore breezes with active leg drive which produced some brilliant play from the likes of Robert Jones and more recently, U.S. Open champion Johnny Miller. However, most amateurs using this method fall short on the demand for precise and repeated timing—because of the shortage of practice opportunities—and they can't control the angle of the flat clubface on a round ball; at least they can't control it reliably, and develop bad habits such as swaying, thereby risking the related disorders of "over-the-top hits" or even shanking.
- The torso swing, which Ben Hogan tapped into after four years of trial and error, made him one of the longest drivers of his day despite the fact that he was only five foot seven inches tall and carried barely 140 pounds on a lean and underfed frame. But it was the resulting repetitiveness of his swing which enabled him to hit fairways and greens with such monotonous regularity that Gene Sarazen, as master of ceremonies for *Shell's Wonderful World of Golf*, was heard to say at Houston Country Club in 1964 after Hogan's match with Sam Snead: "Ben, that was the greatest game of golf I have ever seen. You hit every fairway and every green, and put the ball exactly where you wanted it. Marvelous."

The torso shot is very strong and reliable because of an engagement by the large muscle groups of the abdomen, buttocks, thighs, hips, chest, and upper back, all steered by the shoulders which are connected strongly to the rib cage, and powered by turning the upper body. When connected, these muscle groups offer power, as well as control for the direction of the shot, so much more effectively than do the smaller muscles of hands and arms, because the hands are kept right out of the takeaway, the loading, and the settling into the impact zone. As one pro said after a frustrated search for the secret of Hogan's hand action, "He doesn't swing it! That SOB just hangs onto the club in a death grip!"

Ladies, too, are far better off using the torso for power, because it is more than likely the strongest unit in their body. Perhaps Annika Sorenstam is an exception to this rule, but Babe Didrickson Zaharias, the greatest female athlete of the twentieth century, and Angela Bonallack, twice England's Ladies' Amateur Golf Champion, are testimony to the effectiveness of the rotating torso. The great Babe liked to announce to any audience of ladies, "Just hitch up your girdle and swing those hips."

INTRODUCTION

FINDING THE SOLUTION

I saw Ben Hogan in the flesh only once, but he certainly made a lasting impression. Coming to Vancouver from his victory in the Portland Open in 1945, he had been invited, as a fund-raiser for the war effort, to play an exhibition match at Shaughnessy Heights Golf Course in the residential area of Vancouver.

Sam Snead, Stan Leonard, Fred Wood, and Ben Hogan at Shaughnessy Heights in 1945, having lunch in the men's locker room because professionals were not allowed in the clubhouse in those class-conscious days.

PHOTO CREDIT: Linda Leonard

The sound of the ball cracking off his club split the air like a whip. Spectators were in awe.

Squeezing through the crowd as a twelve-year-old, I moved as close as I could to watch this small but muscular man hit ball after ball, pausing only long enough to announce the club he was about to use and signal his ball shagger to back away. It was an unusually stiff and formal display I thought—none of the usual attempts at humor with trick shots and jokes. But I watched carefully while Hogan put his seven iron back in the bag standing upright beside his caddy. The grooves on the face of the seven iron were worn smooth into a shiny dot resembling a new dime, right on the sweet spot. Every club I could see had that blemish, inflicted no doubt by Mr. Hogan's repeated onslaught to the club's center of gravity. It was amazing to see what I had never seen before . . . or since.

PHOTO CREDIT: B.C. Golf House

Hogan at Shaughnessy Heights in Vancouver, 1945.

Golf has been for me, since then, a love affair of over sixty years, but I wasn't always sure of what the attraction was. Perhaps it was the sense of history felt when walking across the Swilken Burn Bridge to the eighteenth tee at St. Andrews, just as so many historic figures have done for centuries: Tom Auchterlonie, Walter Hagen, Robert Jones, Arnold Palmer, Jack Nicklaus, and Tom Watson. And let's not forget 1995 and the halcyon days for British Open Champion John Daly.

« Sean Connery approaching the fifteenth green at Point Grey golf course in Vancouver, with his Ben Hogan look of determination letting opponents know "This next shot's in the hole, boy."

Maybe it was the breathtaking view of a tee shot across a cove full of wind-whipped Pacific Ocean waves at the sixteenth hole on Cypress Point. But then it could have been the march along the cliffs at Pebble Beach, or the salty wind at Bandon Dunes on the Oregon Coast. Certainly there were the demands of a highly technical game with a hundred variables. Maybe it was all of these marvels which were distractions from the mundanity of life . . . but more than likely, it is the people one meets along the raucous way—and I look back fondly on them all. Like Sir Sean Connery . . . James Bond or Captain Ramius . . . whatever you want to call him. He is the most dedicated golfer I know—and very Hogan-like—with a burning concentration and competitive determination on the course.

The Author's Background: How could an amateur write this book?

When I was ten, my father, like so many at the time, was away at war in Europe where he would spend a total of five and a half years—half my life—so there were no baseball, soccer, or hockey leagues, because there were no coaches and no funding; everyone was working for the war effort, and so for kids, there was not much to do.

Fortunately, I discovered Point Grey golf course on the banks of the Fraser River, alongside Southlands where people kept horse stables just ten minutes from downtown Vancouver. Like Hogan, I was too young to caddy at ten, so hunting golf balls became my new focus. The first ball I found was a Lynx in the rough on the twelfth hole, and I was surprised to hear a woman ask if I was finding any. "Yes," I said quite proudly, and handed her my prize. Again I was surprised when she offered me thirty-five cents, and concluded that I had stumbled upon the key to fortune's door. I began my new trade by understanding where golfers went awry most often and where their abandoned balls might be. I also waded in ditches feeling with my toes for the elusive focus of the game. Then one lucky day, a frightened horse found a way onto the golf course and, stumbling on dangling reins, raced up and down the twelfth fairway and across the green creating considerable damage. Shouting golfers brandishing clubs didn't seem to help the situation, and so I plucked a handful of lush green grass as an offering. The horse came over slowly, and I took hold of the reins. Proudly, I walked him back to the

Blenheim gate and received a pat on the back from the head professional, Duncan Sutherland, and an invitation to caddy when I turned eleven—just as Hogan had done.

As I grew older, my list of loops included some interesting people, some of them highly skilled golfers, all of whom spoke of Ben Hogan in reverential tones. Up for some salmon fishing came Bing Crosby, a four handicap from Hollywood. He paid me well above the dollar fee, handing me a five dollar bill the color of his eyes—blue, like my father's. He reminded me so much of my absent father that I tried to give it back to him. Perhaps he was impressed by my sincere gesture. I don't know, but years later I was invited to his Clambake where I met with many great golfers and characters on the beautiful Monterey Peninsula, a place Ben Hogan loved, and a place where people loved Hogan.

Another loop was "Baby-face" Jimmy McLarnin, the welterweight boxing champion of the world, whose knuckles were so damaged that he had to use a baseball grip. But the most memorable man for whom I caddied was Duncan Sutherland, Point Grey's head professional. Back in 1929, he had paired with Davie Black, the head pro from old Shaughnessy Heights in residential Vancouver. The two home-town boys beat the great Walter Hagen, five-time PGA Championship winner and four-time British Open Champion, who had partnered with Horton Smith, winner of the first Augusta Masters. In this better-ball match, Dunc eagled the fourteenth at Point Grey to go two up, and then closed out the match at seventeen. As they played down eighteen for the benefit of the large gallery, Hagen strolled the fairway with Dunc, who had presented the local fans with a

PHOTO CREDIT: Point Grey GC

Duncan Sutherland (left) on the first tee with Davie Black for their 1929 match against Walter Hagen and Horton Smith.

great game. "How much are they paying you for this?" Hagen asked. The inexperienced Scot shook his head. "Well, I didn't have to work today . . . and there's the dinner . . . with a few drams I'd guess."

Hagen, who travelled the world in a never-ending series of exhibition matches with local pros, nodded wisely, satisfied no doubt with his appearance money of $500. Nevertheless, after dinner, "The Haig" took Dunc's offered hand of farewell, and palmed him a fifty dollar bill. Dunc never forgot that gesture and retold the story many times; so that I began to understand some of the zeitgeist of this game we play and Hogan's place in it.

I also caddied for Ted Kroll, eleven times a winner on the PGA Tour and leading money winner in 1956. He knew Hogan. In fact he played with Hogan in the wildest of all U.S. Opens in 1960 beginning his round with five birdies which drew a nod of approval from the "Ice Man," who was three under par. Nonetheless, this was the season of 1960 at Cherry Hills in Denver, when Arnold Palmer with seven straight birdies would not be denied his first U.S. Open victory. So for Kroll it was "close but no cigar," but he was a player. The thing I remember the most about Kroll was how like Hogan he was when practicing. He would send me out 150 yards for warm-ups, and then hit fifty balls where I wouldn't have to move more than one step to catch the spinning ball in my hand on the first bounce, feeling it sizzle into my palm. When I asked him how he did that, he said only, "Keep your hands solid like Hogan." Years later I was able to interview Kroll during a rain delay of the Seniors Tour at Capilano Golf Club on the North Shore overlooking Vancouver, and I asked him to explain his Hogan remark, which he did—as had other top golfers like Sam Snead, Julius Boros, Mike Souchak, George Knudson, Moe Norman, and Stan Leonard, all in their own slang-ridden, individual way.

PHOTO CREDIT: RCGA

Moe Norman was not hesitant in declaring, "Only two men golfers hit the ball solid every time: Ben Hogan and me." And he may have been right. Sam Snead and Tiger Woods thought so.

Caddying was like watching a parade of highly interesting people demonstrating to observers what they are made of—and how I would have loved to have caddied for Ben Hogan to find out for myself what made him tick. Instead, I spoke to players who had tried, and I was impressed with the devotion and respect they had for someone who no one really understood—even though they had struggled to discover what allowed this smallish man to hit the ball so far and so consistently. It was my good fortune, over the years, to meet these golfers who had played with Hogan, and had studied him. Each one of them left me with a piece of the puzzle regarding the secret that was Hogan's. But in the end, it was a rare opportunity for a game with Moe Norman, the golfing savant, that put it all together for me. This was the player who in eleven years of competitive golf had put only one shot out-of-bounds—and that by only two feet after hitting a summer-hard hillock. He had sixty tournament wins, thirty-three course records, and seventeen holes-in-one.

Moe hit a thousand balls a day, and felt highly complimented when Ben Hogan would watch him practice. Hogan watched only a very few players—George Knudson was one—and none of them for too long . . . but he would watch Moe Norman at length, and Moe was brash enough to declare: "There are only two golfers who can hit a ball solid every time. Only two—and that's Ben Hogan and me."

Moe might have been right, I realized, when Tiger Woods was quoted in *Golf Digest* as saying, "I want to own my own swing. Only two players have ever owned their golf swings. One was Ben Hogan and the other was Moe Norman."

Later that evening after our game, I shagged balls for Moe around the huge putting green at Uplands Golf Club near Victoria, British Columbia. He left a trail of empty Pepsi bottles as I watched him fill each hole with a pyramid of Titleist balls (the only brand he would ever use). I had caddied and shagged for Moe at Point Grey but it was after our game on Vancouver Island that he had somehow accepted me. I had enough nerve to ask, "Shall I shag for you Mr. Norman?"

I was pleased to hear his nonchalant reply: "Sure. Good. That'd be good." It was here he showed me his chips, lobs, and pitches. "Here, watch this, watch this. Hands like Hogan. Hands like steel. A little tip. In she goes."

And then he showed me how it was done.

I was very excited to have Hogan's secret explained to me, but you have to know, that Moe Norman—although well known for his repeating swing—was a bit "different." Like Rain Man, perhaps. Everyone has stories about Moe Norman, the strange and unpredictable golfing savant. Sam Snead regaled Senior Tour colleagues during a rain delay at Capilano on how Moe refused to lay up in front of a creek 235 yards from the tee during a practice round for the Greater Greensboro Open in North Carolina. "Goin' for the bridge. Goin' for the bridge," Moe said, before rolling one of his pipeline drives across the twelve foot wide structure.

Sometimes his oddities weren't so tame. During the CPGA championship in 1969 at Point Grey, I was caddying in the same threesome with Moe. The marshal assigned for crowd control, although a club member, was really just an excited, grinning kid. He kept standing directly behind Moe's ball so that he could look down the target line to follow the shot (as well as check out Norman's very rapid swing). He asked the young marshal several times to move. But before Moe's second shot on the fifth hole, there was the marshal in his vision again. Moe stopped his address and walked back to the marshal standing with his sign while spectators listened: "I know you. Yeah, I know you. You walk like a duck. You dress like a duck. But really, you're not a duck—you're an arsehole. Get out of here!" The marshal disappeared, as the crowd laughed and applauded. Moe's next shot was right beside the pin.

And so as result of his well-known eccentricities, I took Moe's swing revelations to Stan Leonard, one of Canada's greatest competitive golfers. Leonard, like Hogan, was a close-to-the-vest kind of pro, and in a quiet sort of way, he worshiped the great golfer from Texas. Stan was Hogan's size and even dressed with immaculate good taste like the diminutive champion. He approached the game just as Hogan did, and most importantly to me, Stan learned from Hogan how to hit the ball. His peers recognized Leonard as Player of the Year in 1959.

I was fortunate enough to play a lot of twilight summer golf with "Stan the Man" at Point Grey where he was an honorary life member in recognition of his fine competitive record which included eight Canadian PGA championships and an enviable Masters record of which he was justifiably proud after twelve invitations. (He came within a

PHOTO CREDIT: Linda Leonard

Stan Leonard, a Hogan look-alike golf champion who was so like Hogan in appearance, manners, and ball striking ability. Leonard won four PGA events after joining the tour at forty years of age.

putt or two of winning on three separate occasions.) Although Stan stayed with his head professional's job at Marine Drive in Vancouver until he was forty, incredibly, he finally answered his competitive instincts and joined the PGA Tour and was named World Player of the Year in 1959. He recorded wins in the Greater Greensboro Open in 1957, the Tournament of Champions in 1958, and the prestigious Western Open in Chicago in 1960. One of his greatest satisfactions was the fact that Ben Hogan invited him to play in practice rounds. Hogan wouldn't say much. Once at Colonial Golf Club playing with Hogan, Stan threaded a three wood between menacing bunkers on the par five, 575 yard fifteenth hole and "lipped out" his double eagle shot. He missed the eight-foot eagle putt but heard Hogan with rare praise for a fellow competitor: On the way to the next tee Hogan nodded and said, "That was a mighty fine birdie, Stan." Hogan was not given to talking during a game of golf—there was serious work ahead.

Well, that's the way it was with Stan too. As long as I kept my mouth shut, Stan would let me join him during those long summer twilights at Point Grey. We'd hit two balls. Stan would play an imagined game with Ben Hogan; I'd play against Sam Snead.

After my revealing encounter with the eccentric Moe Norman, I cautiously sought the right time to run these revelations past Leonard for what I hoped might be some confirmation. So one day when I spotted Stan on his fitness walk through south Vancouver's well-gardened residential district, I got up enough courage to ask. We stopped at a little park while Stan listened carefully with an occasional nod. We discussed Hogan's foundation, and the connected arm and shoulder structure Hogan called the "Magical Device." Like Moe, George Knudson, and Sam Snead—Stan had his own language to describe the hand action at impact for Hogan's Secret, but they all agreed with Moe concerning the technique. I was now convinced that all the pieces of the puzzle were in place, and hurried down Forty-Ninth Avenue to Point Grey and began practicing. Two weeks later I bettered my age with a sixty-nine. For a senior amateur with responsibilities of career and family plus a diminution of flexibility and strength, I figured that wasn't too bad. I believed that other weekend warriors would like to try Hogan's system for themselves. For those of you who don't know Hogan's story, and even for those who remember the amazing history of a man who "dragged himself up by his own bootstraps," let's quickly review his record, and then we'll begin.

CHAPTER 1

FROM RUDE BEGINNINGS

Ben Hogan didn't stand a chance for a successful life as a kid from the plateau lands of central Texas. He was born on August 13, 1912, in Stephenville Hospital across the Brazos River from Fort Worth, just ten miles north from his family's simple cottage in a cattle town named Dublin. His mother, Clara, married a blacksmith named Chester who had health problems on top of the bad luck to be caught in the middle of a horse-dominated economy changing inexorably into an automobile economy. Depressed and impoverished, Chester could not cope with all the changes which were beyond his control, and so chose a cold and brittle St. Valentine's Day to shoot himself in front of his quiet and polite nine-year-old son Bennie. The noise of the thirty-eight caliber pistol aimed awkwardly at the heart in the confines of a tiny cottage blew away for young Ben any hope of a life which could be supported by normal amounts of trust and confidence.

It should be noted that, in contrast, Tiger Woods's father, Earl Woods, was a decorated Green Beret with two tours in Vietnam. So, as a lieutenant colonel, he knew the value of discipline and commitment. His goal was to transfer to his son the essential characteristics of a good person as well as those of a champion by self-examination and discovery of one's talent, and the unwavering determination to polish it. Tiger's daily routine began with making his bed every morning then

A watercolor of Hogan displaying the balance and grace of the best ball striker in golf, just after his 1953 U.S. Open win. But he did not start out as such—far from it.

finishing his homework before any golf could be contemplated.

Earl would deliberately try to intimidate his young son while playing golf. "Water on the right, OB on the left," he would point out just before Tiger's downswing. "He would look at me with the most evil look," Earl recalled, "but he wasn't permitted to say anything."

"One day I did all my tricks, and he looked at me and just smiled . . . . 'Tiger,' I said, 'you've completed your training.' And I made him a promise: 'You'll never run into another person as mentally tough as you.'"

Things were quite different for Bennie, the baby of his family. He moved with his older sister Princess and brother Royal to Fort Worth, where his mother tried to hold the stricken family together as a seamstress. Royal left school to help support the family as a delivery boy, while his little brother Bennie sold newspapers. At eleven, Ben began caddying at Glen Garden for sixty-five cents a loop—even though it meant a seven mile round-trip from home and back.

Never a dedicated student because of his need to earn money, Hogan dropped out of Central High School in Fort Worth in 1930 to turn professional for the Texas Open in San Antonio at age seventeen. Because of a terrible hook, he struggled ineffectively for eight frustrating and challenging years, and then forced himself by sheer willpower and tenacity to invent a swing that would not let him down—like people including his father were capable of doing. He knew he needed something that would control the ball's direction. Something that would take the fear out of important and dangerous shots. Then after inventing "arduous daily practice" and after experimenting daily through hours of intense and concentrated ball striking—he honed a new swing through trial and error.

Just as important, Hogan met a young woman named Valerie Fox in a Fort Worth Sunday school, and found at last someone upon whom he could depend. He had developed a protective and distrustful personality both on and off the course. However, despite his demons and down to their last few dollars, Hogan went on the tour again in one last desperate gamble to earn a living from the "Gold Trail" during the Great Depression—and finally won $1,100 paired with Vic Ghezzi at the 1938 Four Ball Invitation in Hershey, Pennsylvania. By 1940 he had won three events in a row in North Carolina. The struggle appeared to have been won.

Looking back in a 1982 interview strangely evocative of Earl Woods's view of determination, Ben Hogan was to say:

> "I feel sorry for rich kids now. I really do. Because they're never going to have the opportunity I had. Because I knew tough things. And I had a tough day all my life and I can handle tough things. They can't. And every day that I progressed was a joy to me, and I recognized it every day. I don't think I could have done what I've done if I hadn't had the tough days to begin with."

Tiger Woods has said, "Ben Hogan was the greatest driver there ever was," and undoubtedly recognized that Ben Hogan's toughness in competition might have matched his own . . . and wouldn't that be a battle to watch?

Further, as majestic as Tiger's short game can be, a lot of golfers forget that Hogan's short game system made him an exceptional player around the greens. For example, Kevin Riley, a golf pro who still works for the Ben Hogan Company, remembers in 1955 when Mr. Hogan went to the pro-am for the Los Angeles Open at Inglewood Country Club. Kevin sat with Lloyd Mangrum, U.S. Open winner in 1946, and recalls a shot Hogan made at the par four eighteenth hole. The final hole had an elevated green with approximately eight degrees of slope to receive the second shot. Hogan appeared to be in big trouble when his ball took a strange bounce and went over the back of the green and down a slight hill. With the gallery watching anxiously, Hogan lobbed from over back of the green to a putting surface sloping away from him. The ball took one hop next to the hole,

PHOTO CREDIT: Mike Lilly

Here is another solid-looking stance by Tiger Woods, the man chasing Ben Hogan's records. The clubhead is hovering for an unrestricted and controlled takeaway. Caddy Steve Williams checks his alignment.

bounced past the cup, then put on the brakes, and backed up the eight-degree slope to stop within two feet of the hole. Kevin had been sure the ball would roll over the front edge of the green, but no, it was another spectacular shot. "That's Hogan," Mangrum said. "He does stuff that no one else can."

Ben Hogan was also a great putter who played through major championships such as the Masters and PGA without a single three putt. It is worth paying attention to his instruction.

Before we look at Ben Hogan's system for a solid short game, let's first check the record he earned without the benefit of junior development programs or college leagues.

BEN HOGAN'S EARLY CAREER TOUR VICTORIES:

1938: Hershey Four Ball (with Vic Ghezzi).

1940: North and South Open, Greater Greensboro Open, Asheville Open, Goodall Palm Beach Round Robin.

1941: Asheville Open, Chicago Open, Hershey Open, Miami Biltmore Four Ball (with Gene Sarazen), Inverness Four Ball (with Jimmy Demaret).

1942: Los Angeles Open, San Francisco Open, North and South Open, Asheville Open, Hale American Open, Rochester Open.

1945: Nashville Invitational, Portland Open, Richmond Invitational, Montgomery Invitational, Orlando Open.

1946: Phoenix Open, San Antonio Open, St. Petersburg Open, Miami International Four Ball (with Jimmy Demaret), Colonial Invitational, Western Open, Goodall Championship, Winnipeg Open, PGA Championship, Golden State Open, Dallas Invitational, North and South Open, Inverness Four Ball (with Jimmy Demaret).

1947: Los Angeles Open, Phoenix Open, Colonial Invitational, Chicago Victory Open, World Championship of Golf, Miami International Four Ball (with Jimmy Demaret), Inverness Four Ball (with Jimmy Demaret).

1948: Los Angeles Open, PGA Championship, U.S. Open, Inverness Four Ball (with Jimmy Demaret), Motor City Open, Reading Open, Western Open, Denver Open, Reno Open, Glendale Open.

1949: Bing Crosby Pro-Am, Long Beach Open.

Hogan and his wife, Valerie, his true pal, were on top of the world at the height of his career in 1949. He appeared to have conquered his demons after adjusting his "caddy swing" grip and polishing his competitive game through the relentless grind of hitting practice balls, forever his favorite pastime. He and Valerie were now in a brand new Cadillac heading to El Paso on a misty February afternoon.

Ben drove cautiously in the fog, but fate had arranged it so he would meet a ten ton Greyhound bus just as the twenty-seven-year-old substitute bus driver chose to pass a truck on a two-lane bridge at fifty miles per hour trying to make up lost time. *The St. Petersburg Times* reported that he was found guilty and fined twenty-five dollars. (Two years later when the driver was involved in a similar accident in which two people died, the bus company finally apologized to the Hogans. Valerie gave them an earful about what she thought of their delinquency.)

As depicted in the bio-picture *Follow the Sun*, Hogan threw himself across Valerie to protect her. The engine came through the dashboard and smashed his left ankle, crushed his leg, and fractured his pelvis. His left eye was severely damaged when smashed by the dashboard—damage which in later life, combined with aging, seriously limited his depth perception. Doctors told Valerie that he might never walk again, let alone play golf.

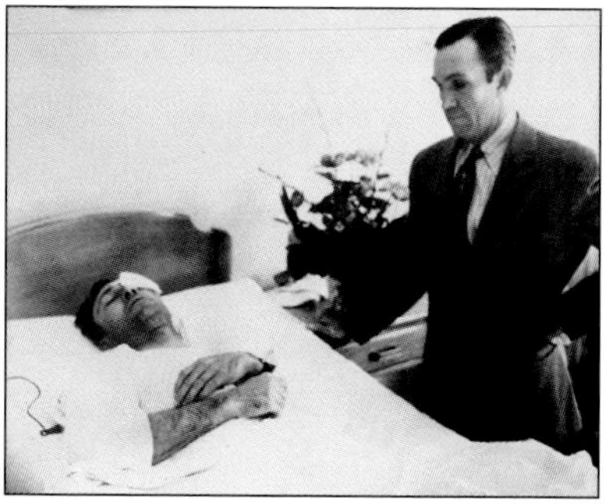

PHOTO CREDIT: Associated press

The deeply distressed champion golfer is visited by his brother Royal. Later Jimmy Demaret found Hogan practicing "ceiling putts" while in his hospital bed and was determined to nominate Hogan as captain of the U.S. Ryder Cup team.

Hospitalized for two months, and undergoing complex and dangerous surgery, Hogan battled pain, blood clots, and depression, but still he hung in there. On April 1, 1949, Valerie took Ben home—now weighing only 120 pounds—with pain in his left shoulder and leg that would be a burden for the rest of his days. Golf was out of the question . . . or was it?

Seven months after the accident, Hogan went to England as the non-playing captain of the U.S. Ryder Cup Team. Upon his return home in September, he began to hit balls again with a stiff-legged swing, and when he had developed it enough, he decided to try it out at the Los Angeles Open that winter. His weight was up to 160 pounds (partially at least, a result of muscle mass from his rigorous rehabilitation schedule). To everyone's surprise, and in spite of the elastic bandages encasing his legs, he tied for first place—only to lose to Sam Snead in a Monday morning play-off. The good news was that he was back in the game. For Hogan it was also a sign that, if he could tolerate the pain, he could compete on a shortened schedule of tournaments.

The 1950 United States Open was held in June at the Merion Golf Club in Ardmore, Pennsylvania, where Hogan hit a classic one iron to within two feet of the eighteenth green to set up a win which noted sportswriter Dan Jenkins would call "the most incredible comeback in the history of sports."

Jack Nicklaus summarized his thoughts with this statement:

"So many things about Hogan were special. He was the greatest shot-maker I ever saw. He was more determined and could totally out-focus anyone else in his time of playing. No one seemed to know him very well, which made him that much more feared as a competitor. He probably worked harder than anyone to reach the top, and it took him a long time. Then, when he got there, his body was all but destroyed by the car accident. All he did was start over again at nearly forty, and got even better. Nobody was like Hogan."

Hogan's own reaction was "It proved that I could still play," and he began to increase his workload, honing his new swing which now had reduced leg action, but involved a muscular connection between the shoulders, arms, and torso that Hogan called his Magical Device. He also let it be known that somewhere within the confusion of his high speed swing there was a move he announced as his "Secret." It became evident that these two components proved to be highly effective, because Hogan put together a record of championships which took him, once again, to the top of the PGA tour:

BEN HOGAN'S POST ACCIDENT TOUR VICTORIES:

1950: U.S. Open.

1951: The Masters, U.S. Open, World Championship of Golf.

1952: Colonial National Invitational.

1953: The Masters, Pan American Open, Colonial National Invitational, U.S. Open, British Open (at Carnoustie).

1959: Colonial National Invitational. Following his post accident wins in the 1953 Masters, the U.S. Open, and the British Open at Carnoustie, Scotland—*Life* magazine printed a description of "Hogan's Secret" in its August 8, 1955, issue.

Readers gobbled it up. Unfortunately, Hogan's artist, the highly skilled Anthony Ravielli, may not have understood golf as well as he sketched anatomical illustrations. Or perhaps it was Hogan himself who did not fully understand some of the terms being used. Or maybe it was because, as Tiger states, "Feel is not real." Whatever the reason, there was mislabeling of some of Hogan's actions, so that Hogan did not explain the secret correctly, and confusion reigned. Many a teaching pro will laughingly agree that Hogan made them a lot of money as they tried to correct the damage done by the misdirection.

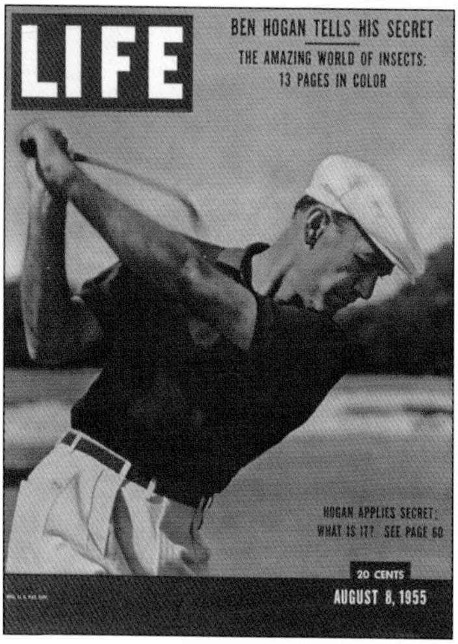

PHOTO CREDIT: Getty Images

Life magazine August 8, 1955. Ben Hogan at the top of his backswing and once again on top of his game.

Hogan himself admitted: "I doubt if it will be worth a doggone to the weekend duffer, and it might ruin a bad golfer."

Mr. Hogan planned to clarify the misleading information and the several tantalizing hints he left behind. Unfortunately, before he could be persuaded to properly describe his secret and how to apply it while using the correct anatomical terms, he passed away, leaving hundreds of analysts puzzling for over fifty years. At least thirty pros put pens to paper with "answers" ranging from the way he positioned his feet at address to the way he waggled his ultra-stiff clubs. One pro provided a puzzling theory: "Hogan was truthful when he emphasized the cupping of his wrist. But, as he was later to reveal to a friend, it was only part of the story. The other part was the correct functioning of his right knee. The wrist was cupped because that was the only position it could assume based on the right knee's position."

Golfing giant Gene Sarazen summarized the wide variety of opinions about Hogan's Secret by tapping his head with the observation that "Hogan had it up here."

I had the temerity to describe, in universal anatomical language, what was taught to me in slang terms by Moe Norman and Stan Leonard with snippets from all the other professional golfers (George Knudson, Alvie Thompson, Jack Nicklaus, Ernie Brown, and various caddies) who shared their knowledge and experiences with Hogan for a book titled *Ben Hogan's Magical Device and the Secret Within*. I now present an illustrated account of Hogan's short game system, wherein his secret move at impact is well described and illustrated.

Some of you will have a sound understanding of Ben Hogan's fundamentals. If that's the case, then you should turn straight to Chapter Two: Putting with the Magical Device, because putting was not in Hogan's famous book, *Five Lessons*. However, if you want a quick review of Hogan's unique and well-studied basic positions, perhaps a fast read is a good idea—turn to Chapter Eighteen.

Ben Hogan protégé Stan Leonard applying the secret to solid impact.

PHOTO CREDIT: Marine Drive GC

Hogan spent four years of trial and error developing his graceful and balanced swing. Every variation has a reason for being there and perhaps is worth consideration. Fortunately, his basic action of the Magical Device and the application of his secret applies to most good setups, so you won't be asked to abandon your swing entirely. Even if you add just the Magical Device you'll be much better off. And if you want to move on from there, you will be ready to build into the correct application of his secret.

SOME TERMS YOU WILL NEED

Before any serious discussion can begin on a serious topic, we must define and agree on the use of terminology so that communication has at least a chance of clarity. Mr. Hogan knew, and had great confidence in, what he was doing and what techniques he used in order to swing the club so repetitively into the ball. But how can we communicate these thoughts and feelings repeated so often in hours

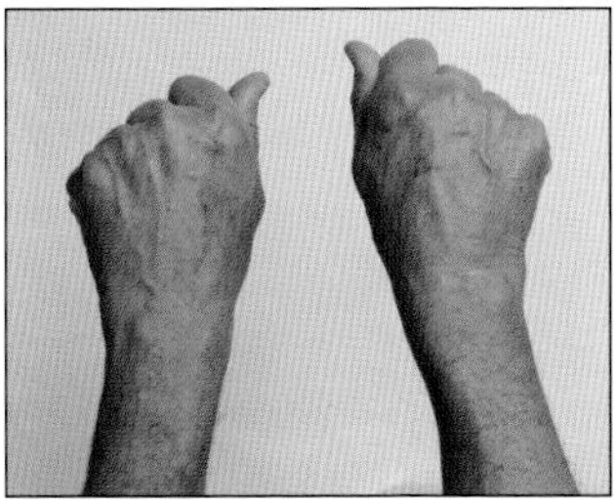

Pronation. From a "palms up" position, rotating the hands and forearms inward to face down.

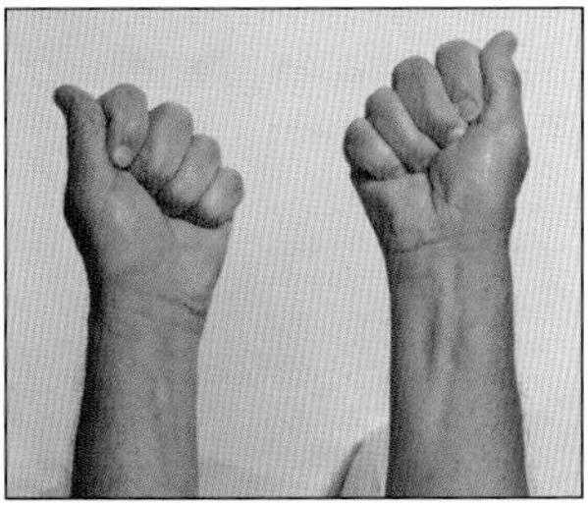

Supination. From a "palms down" position, rotating the hands and forearms outward to face up.

PHOTO CREDIT: Pacific Press

Jock Mackinnon at Shaughnessy Heights Golf Club in Vancouver circa 1946. Note the old Scottish splayed-foot stance with the pronated right hand and arm through the impact zone. The left arm is collapsing and the left hand is no doubt collapsing as well. That's the way the old-time players did it . . . and if you had super timing or hand-eye coordination—as Jock had—you could mostly get away with it. However, the predilection to hook the ball was not kind to scorecards, and when the golfer flinched to block the pronation, the ball was often into trees on the right.

Dorsiflexion. Raising the top of the hand alone as if to touch knuckles to the wrist produces a concave or cupped wrist.

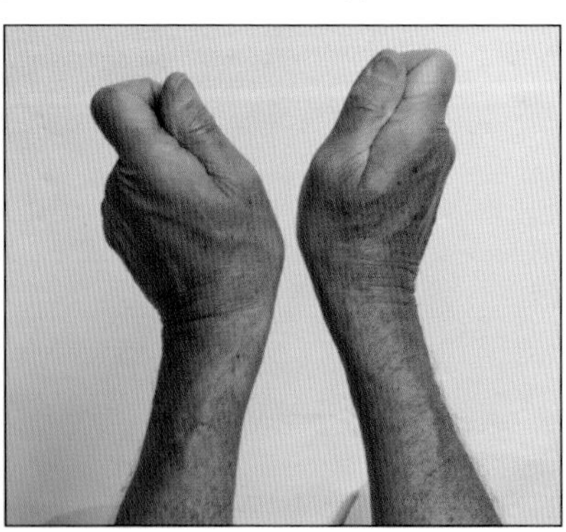

Palmar flexion. Curling the palm into itself as if to make a fist produces a convex or bowed wrist with an arch.

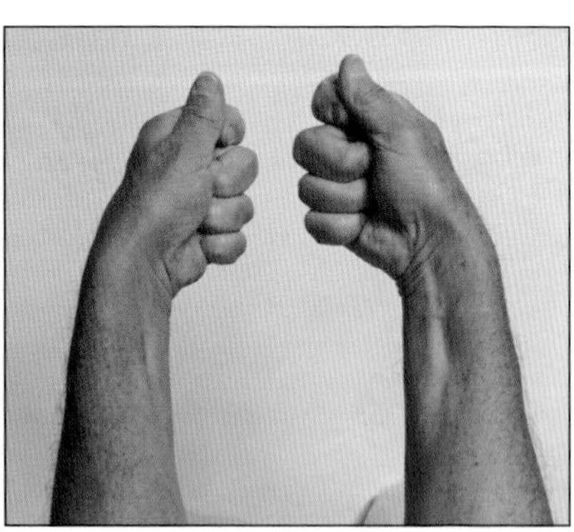

of practice in an era where a couple of putts and shoulder stretches seemed to do the trick for everyone else but Hogan?

It has become apparent to more and more golf analysts that Mr. Hogan did not use universally accepted definitions for some of his physical actions, and that was a problem for many golfers who tried to emulate his great swing but unfortunately discovered only new ways to snap-hook or shank the ball.

Here are some basic terms we shall use in describing the Magical Device and the secret within.

PRONATION AND SUPINATION

Mr. Hogan spoke about pronation on the backswing and then, after the downswing, supination on the forward swing into the ball—but there is no clear direction as to how he wanted golfers to achieve this. Which hand was he talking about? At what stage do you pronate or supinate? With the whole arm? Besides, this was not the action within his Magical Device. In fact, it is precisely with these issues that the confusion surrounding the secret lies.

It should be noted that a golfer can supinate or pronate only one hand at a time. The unwary player would pronate his left hand on the takeaway, which would open the blade ("lay the club off") with the risk of getting the club "stuck behind" him at the top. In a desperate attempt to square the club at impact, the golfer might pronate the right hand without the hope of getting things back to "square" with any regularity. Tiger Woods

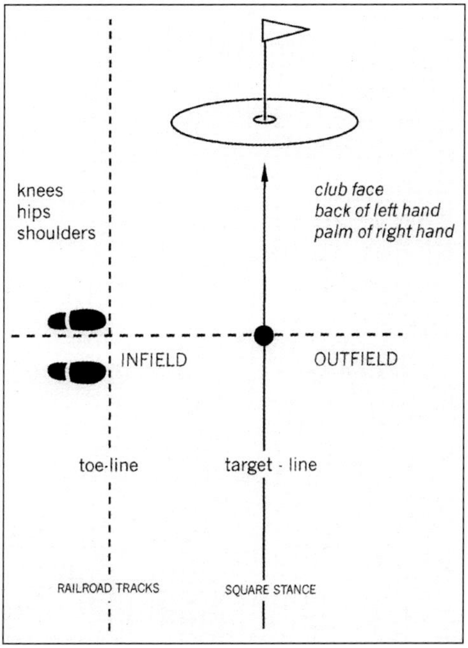

Diagram of lines for "railroad tracks" alignment.

calls this action "flipping" and warns young golfers who use the wrists in their attempt to get extra distance that they are heading for control problems with devastating results at times. Besides, Hogan did not flip or pronate, as you shall see.

MORE TERMS FOR THE PURPOSES OF THIS BOOK

- **Antecubital fossa:** Let's call them dimples, located at the inside of the elbow on each arm.
- **Iliac crest:** The forward-most edge of the pelvic girdle, just above, and inside, the hip joint. As you will see, Hogan wanted the two elbows to be fairly close together at address and impact. Although we know that the contact point is more to the crest of the pelvis, let's agree to call this spot "the waist area."
- **Over the top:** When, from the highest point of the backswing, the right shoulder moves over the ball to the outfield beyond. This happens because without settling into the bar-stool position as the first move down from the top, the golfer hits from the top and the left shoulder pulls away from the target line at the start of the downswing instead of rising up vertically so that the right shoulder can come under the chin to pass between the stance line and the target line on the "infield" side of the ball.
- **Under the ball:** When the hands, right shoulder, and right knee move the clubhead to impact from the infield side of the target line.
- **Sternum:** The flat, bony structure in the center of the chest.
- **Left brain thinking:** Where facts rule; detail oriented; words and numbers are memorized for conscious recall. Think quiz show participants. This book will require a little left brain work such as the "alignment checklist." On the course, your conscious mind takes in facts—two-club wind, down hill lie, etc.—and then, when ready for the actual shot, transfers control to the right side of the brain for visualization of the ball's flight to its target. (I've noticed that surgeons, dentists, carpenters, and trick-shot golfers are good at this switching back and forth.)
- **Right brain thinking:** Where imagination rules; big picture orientation; symbols and images are remembered within a context. Golf is a game where you have to put your right brain to work—uninterrupted by the left side—because when you visualize the flight of the ball, there is nothing but the target

spot on the green in your subconscious picture. (There are of course silly twits who think they are very clever by pointing out something negative in your path, expecting you to be distracted by their observation. Give them the blank stare, and the rhetorical question, they deserve: "What lake?")

- **Target line:** The imaginary line drawn in your mind from your ball to the flag-stick. There is nothing negative in this vision as in a lake or a trap.
- **Toe line or stance line:** The imaginary line drawn across the golfer's shoes towards the target, and parallel to the target line.
- **Fulcrum:** The point upon which a lever turns, or where the lever is supported in its function of moving the lever.
- **Sweet spot:** The invisible center of gravity located in the absolute weight neutral center of a golf ball or clubhead.

CHAPTER 2

PUTTING WITH HOGAN'S SYSTEM

THE SPECIFIC PROBLEM:

How did Hogan impact the ball so solidly and so consistently?

GETTING STARTED WITH SHORT PUTTS

It goes without saying that you want to start hitting the long ball with the system that made Ben Hogan the most accomplished striker of the ball in the history of golf. Nevertheless, described below is the quickest and most assured way of absorbing his swing details in a permanent and reflexive way, so that you don't have to analyze every move before you give the ball a whack. Please take a little time—it has a minimum of organization—and learn how to use the triangle of arms and shoulders that Hogan called his Magical Device. You may be "a good putter." So was I. But when I took the seven days required to learn the system described below, my average putts per round dropped from thirty-three to twenty-seven. As you will no doubt agree, the latter number is much more acceptable; it moves you from the eighties to the seventies with ease. But of course I can't force anyone. A longtime athletic rugby friend of mine struggles to break ninety but won't try the Magical Device because he "already putts well enough." I try to emphasize that putting with the triangle used properly is the structural basis for the rest of your shots as well.

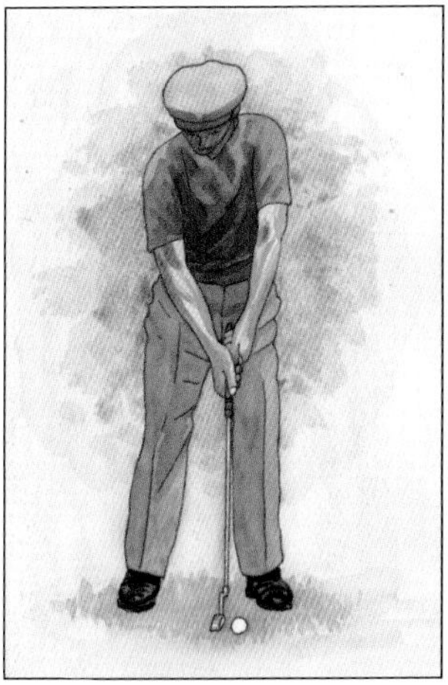

Ben Hogan at the address position for putting. You can see where the influence for Ben Crenshaw, and the new style of Phil Mickelson, comes from.

Ben Hogan put his swing together by dint of hard work after literally starving during his third attempt to earn a living as a touring golf professional in the "hard old-days" of the Dirty Thirties. Traveling in California in 1937 with his new bride Valerie, and down to their last few dollars, Hogan stole oranges from the groves in the land of plenty in order to keep on going. Finally he captured his first big check—$385—in the Oakland Open. He got to that point only after teaching himself a repeating "power fade" so that he knew where the ball was going.

The key to getting to this point of control consisted of two factors: A determination to escape a horrifying childhood in the badlands of Texas and the fear of failure. With a dose of desperation, he began a fanatic's schedule of daily practice which went on for years from morning 'til night in an attempt to "get a hold on" the details of "chess on grass" and the quest to control each shot with precision.

I'm not assured that you are in a position to follow such a regime.

However, the absence of the regular habit of pounding five hundred balls per day should not keep you from playing decent golf. You might not be able to play golf every day—let alone play all year round. Still, you need to learn a system for golf—not just a few tips from the cognoscenti or some Band-Aids from friends.

I would like to point out, as gently as possible, that the Magical Device moves you skillfully from putting, through chipping and lobs, to longer shots where Hogan's Secret is to be applied. You really should study this structure very carefully.

This connection and special placement of hands, arms, and shoulders is what Hogan playfully named his "Magical Device" when questioned about the technique which allowed him to control the direction of the ball so well. Notice the position of the left arm locked in supination, thus preventing any rolling of the arm and the resultant closing of the club's face. The right elbow is connected to the waist area.

The easiest and fastest way to arrive successfully at this structurally powerful impact point—please humor me—is to learn and ingrain the function of the Magical Device while putting and chipping so that Hogan's Secret can be applied to longer shots without reviewing a dozen details as you try to remember the process. You want to stay away from a dark domain known as "paralysis by analysis." You need to be tilting this triangle from "learned habit" so that you can visualize your ball's flight to the target (and not worry about what is happening to your body) in order to have the club's face direct the ball along that line. When you finish the first week working with the triangle, you will already be proficient in putting and chipping—which is, after all, an important percentage of your total game.

Hogan stated boldly: "There is no reason why an average golfer can't get a lot better and break eighty if he just uses this technique." And he meant it.

Well I used it, and am very glad I did. On a chilly morning this past fall I was not playing very well, but one-putted the first seven holes to save my skin. One of my worthy opponents said on the seventh green, "If you sink this one, that putter goes where the sun don't shine."

The charm of that remark—if indeed charm is the word—is that while working on the Hogan method of putting I proved to myself that the putter did not matter. I got to the point where I had rolled twenty six-foot putts in a row over a dime on my basement carpet, and wondered if it was the putter. I changed to another and hit the dime with the next twenty balls, then switched to a third putter and hit it twenty more times in a row. "It ain't the arrow, it's the Indian."

But I digress: The point is that I did the drill and it works. So please try it—thirty to forty repetitions a day for seven days. If it snows where you live, you can afford the time well spent.

The main point of Ben Hogan's putting stroke is to be found in the special connection of the arms to the torso; this base acts as a solid, stable, and stationary unit during the stroke. And the best way to practice forming this highly effective structure is right in front of a full-length mirror without a putter or ball. There is no need to travel all the way to a practice area, either.

It is important to do this drill—which might at first seem a little lame—because you get the feel of this action without any notion of memorizing rules. Performing the action will give you context for remembering—especially with the added senses required to critique your balance and stability as you watch in the mirror. This is not a "golf by numbers" type of activity.

With a high arch in the address position, point the fingers down to an imaginary ball opposite the heel of your left foot which is bearing ninety percent of your weight. It doesn't matter too much where your right foot is. Hogan put it well behind him and far away from the target line. The beauty of having your weight on one foot is that it determines where the bottom of your swing's arc will be. This will become important later on as we talk about iron play.

Oh yes, the bony point of your right elbow should be resting on the appendix area, just above and inside your hip joint. When "connected" like this to a stable lower body, the right forearm becomes a fulcrum which will guide the right hand precisely and consistently back to the address position.

The left elbow's dimple points upward toward the sky. The effect is that the left arm is held in a stable position so that the left hand does not "roll over." The desired result is that the back of the left hand points straight toward the target.

To begin the backswing for a six-foot putt, move the imaginary club away from the imaginary ball by

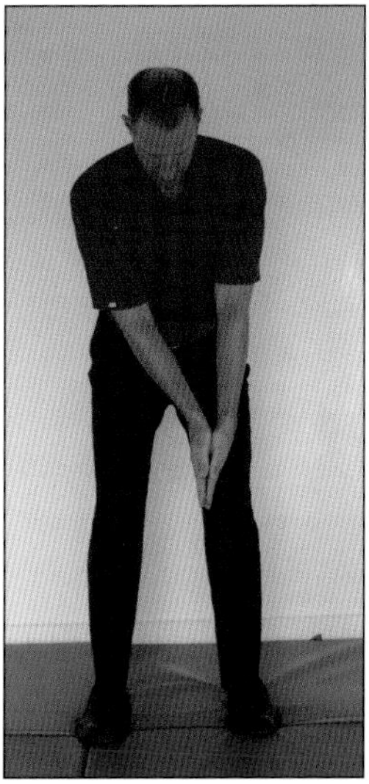

Place your hands together in the address position without a club.

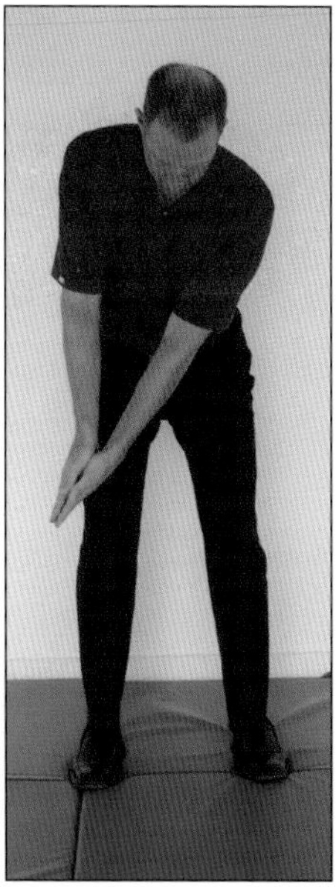
Hands-only take away action without a club.

pushing the heel of the left hand against the heel of the right hand by lowering the left shoulder; if you have "attached" the shoulder to the upper left arm properly—by squeezing the left armpit to the upper rib cage (the left elbow can be a few inches away clear of the chest)—this lowering will push the arm holding the putter back along the target line away from the ball.

Watch yourself in the mirror to see that nothing below the waist moves. As a matter of fact, you will notice as you tip the Magical Device (i.e., "the triangle") that even the hands—or should I say especially the hands—don't move. The hands go where the connected triangle guides them. And the head doesn't move either. Look in the mirror to watch what happens. You should see that the back of your leading left hand is slightly angled and looking down at the floor. The point is you haven't moved your hands by rolling them, as happens when pronating the left hand. (Hogan didn't do that either—except when he "waggled" his club before long shots. But you will see that this waggle was employed for a completely different purpose, and gave a lot of people a completely wrong impression of how he took the club away from the ball—but more about that later.)

To return the hands to the imaginary ball, simply raise the left shoulder; watch in the mirror as the hands return to the address position and the imagined ball. The shoulders tilt on a plane that is parallel to the target line. (It gets a little different for the full shot as you will see in due course.)

For now, your focus is that there should be no movement of the hands by themselves. The hands are still arched and hold on to the angles positioned at address. The left hand has a palmar (convex) flex toward the target. The right hand is held in dorsiflexion (concave) but arched position.

Keep raising the left shoulder and watch the hands sweep rhythmically over where a ball would be. The left elbow dimple is pointed to the sky—this prevents any roll-over of the arm—so that the face of the putter remains square to the target line. This square position indicates where the ball will be heading.

Don't be surprised if the bony point of the right elbow is pulled away from the crest of the pelvis and slides across the abdomen a couple of inches toward the navel. The elbow is still touching the rib cage of the torso, and so hasn't become "disconnected."

Now, for the next two days, your task is to repeat tilting the triangle through thirty imaginary six-foot putts, so that the triangle moves your hands by means of the connected and solid arms, hands, and shoulders. Your hands don't even twitch.

Arnold Palmer was telling us this back in the 1960s. Some people didn't listen then, and you might be tempted to back out now to avoid screwing up your own pristine putting stroke. "But my old swing feels comfortable," you say. Of course it does, you've never changed it. But it still offers no better than thirty-six putts per round—that's why you have to try Hogan's technique for one week. The good news is that this method isn't a disease. Try it in the middle of winter if you're worried that you won't be able to find your way back to your comfortable old style swing. I am reminded of the mother of a fifteen-year-old high school boy who had just begun a weight training unit in school scheduled for one month. She wanted her son excused from PE class, "Before he becomes muscle-bound."

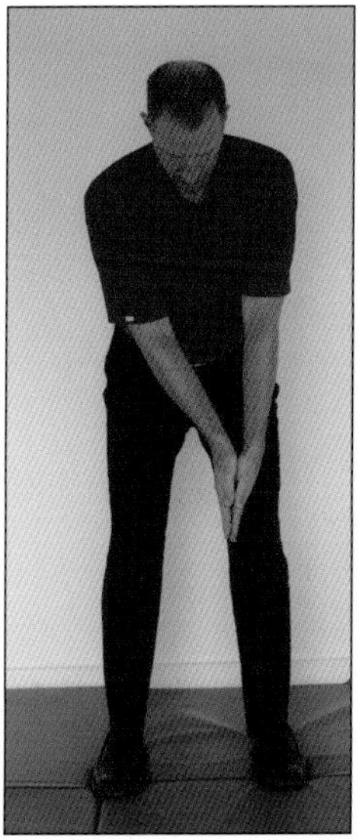

Hands to impact.

Hands swing through.

Points to watch:

- Your knees remain slightly flexed.
- Both hands are arched.
- The left hand is bulging (convex) to the target.
- The right hand remains cupped (concave) throughout the tilt.
- Posture: shoulders back.

The fingers never move in this palms-together drill—especially those of the right hand which are capable of collapsing the leading left hand during a full swing at a golf ball. (Again, more on this later.) For the next two days, do your "hands only" mirror drill whenever and wherever you can (men's washrooms are not a preferred site, although observers do catch on pretty quick).

When you are tilting regularly, without moving anything other than the triangle—be aware of some other details. For example, feel the heels of the hands pressing together throughout the tilt. This adds to the strength of the hand structure but does not involve the fingers which are quite relaxed. Then try the same drill with the hands in the regular grip—use a short stick if you want—and squeeze the last three fingers of the left and and feel the solid sensation of a "well-connected" triangle.

The main thing is to adjust to the notion that you are not going to move your hands during the putting stroke, because hinging hands—which alters the clubface—are usually the culprits in a missed putt.

When you can use the triangle properly in front of the mirror without any equipment and without moving your hands or fingers, it's probably time to try tilting the triangle with a putter. Not to be picky . . . but a blade putter is probably the best putter to work with. The mallet putter is quite distracting (and some of the newer models are bizarre). Hogan liked simplicity in color and design, and would never have anything more distracting than a plain blade like the Acushnet Bulls Eye—a simple piece of great-feeling brass clubhead. Hogan was the same way with shoes—they were never to be a distraction—he had them handmade of plain brown or black leather in London for $1,200 a pair, with an extra cleat in the center of his foot for traction. However, he certainly knew where the sweet spot on his putter was, and sometimes had it marked with a small sight line or dot.

Tap to find the sweet spot.

Most good putters prefer that the palms face one another, and that both thumbs press down to the ball when putting. Hogan advised that both hands should arch, to simulate the preferred

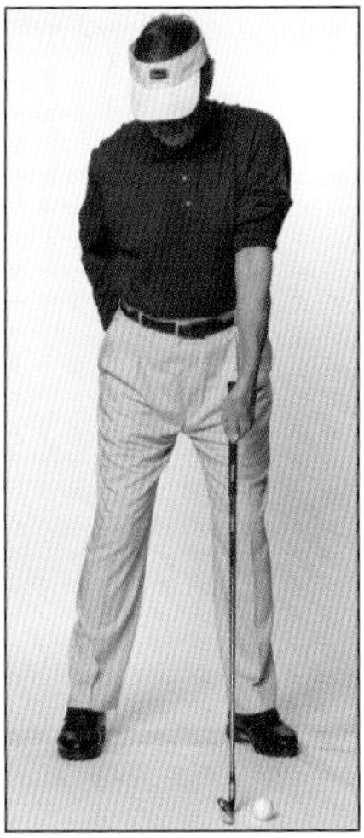

The long left thumb which weakens the grip to avoid rolling the hand into impact.

impact position for the hands, as the club sweeps through the ball's sweet spot.

At address, stand with your toe line parallel to the target line. You can experiment with different stances later, but for now keep the lines across your toes, knees, hips, and shoulders all square and parallel to the target line. Please note that the putter blade is hovering—and we should discuss this point.

When a golfer puts the club on the ground, it feels so secure . . . but if ever there was a false sense of security, the club on the ground is it. A basic insecurity about your performance will cause tension . . . and the more important the putt, the more tension. This usually means a too speedy flick-up of the putter resting on the green with a tendency to push it inside the target line, or worse, outside. The speed of the takeaway from a grounded club is usually too fast, which in turn encourages a "deceleration" into the ball—and you often wind up short of the hole.

A putter held above the ground is moved smoothly away from the ball in a pure pendulum swing by the shoulder tilt, and moved smoothly back, without alteration of the clubface by independent hand movement.

The Hogan system will take you to new heights of confidence, so try this method—you could learn to love it. Hover the clubhead for a smooth and rhythmical takeaway from the ball, powered by tilting the triangle.

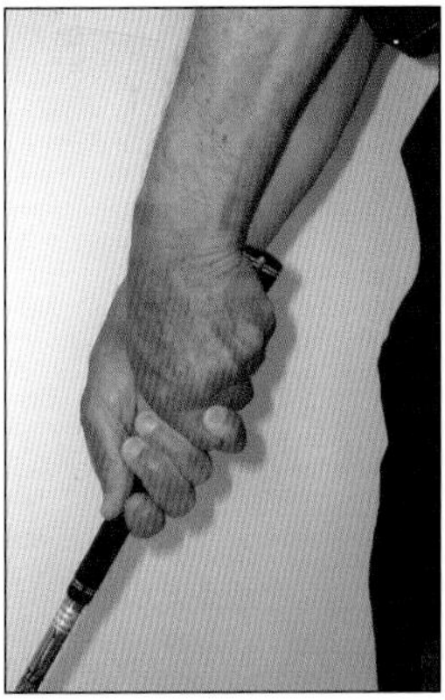

The putting grip. Many variations exist of course, but Hogan wanted the impact position to be sturdy, with thumbs pointing down to the ball and the hands arched for strength of the structural unit. So, a good way to feel it is to assume the position at address—and simply come back to it for impact. Give it a week's trial.

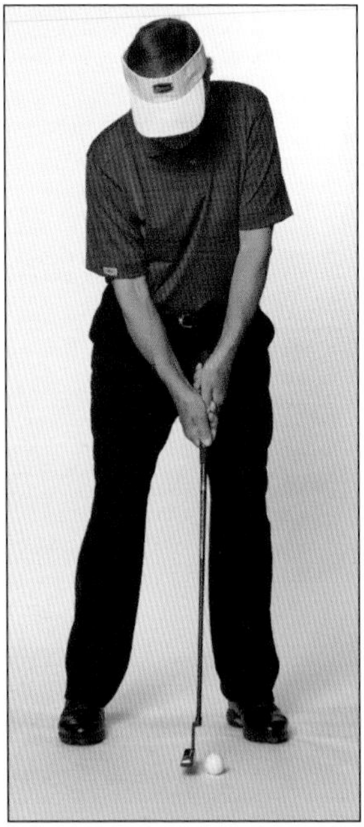

The upper arms are "connected" to the torso. The arched left hand is ahead of the ball at address and will remain ahead through impact—especially if the model points the dimple on the inside of his left elbow to the sky. Experiment with the ball position. Hogan had it just in front of his left toe. The bottom of the arc is where the body's weight settles.

You'll soon agree with Hogan that it is indeed a Magical Device.

On the Pebble Beach putting green, I remember Jack Nicklaus practicing after dinner the evening before the final round of the 1982 U.S. Open, in which Nicklaus, the four-time U.S. Open Champion, was in contention once again. I watched as he chose a cup on a sidehill, to then begin stroking five-foot putts from the right side. Thirty putts were gathered and tossed back by his caddy (perhaps Angelo Argea, but I can't recall). After the first set of thirty, Nicklaus switched to the other side to hit another thirty balls.

Why was I not surprised the next day when he charged into the lead with five straight birdies? Then there was another birdie opportunity on the eighteenth at the edge of the Pacific Ocean—wouldn't you know—a five-foot sidehiller.

With scarcely a pause, a very confident Nicklaus moved into position and stroked the ball into the back of the cup—the leader in the clubhouse in line for his fifth U.S. Open title (more on this later). It was an impressive putting afternoon.

The takeaway with putter. The back of the left hand is pointing down toward the ground. It has not rolled in pronation. Neither hand moved by itself.

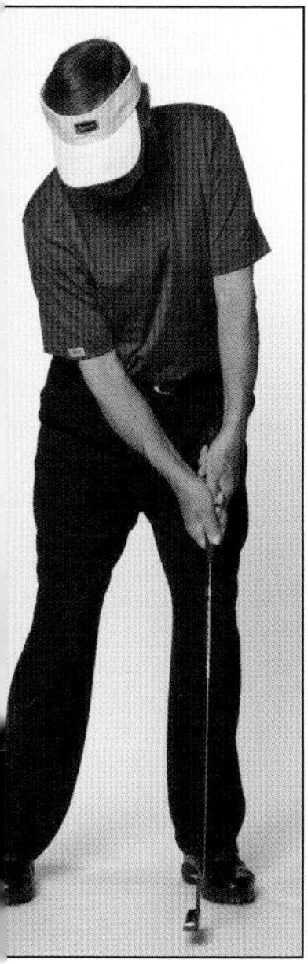

« It's the address position all over again. The left elbow dimple should be pointed at the sky.

Hands have not moved » from their original position and are still in front of the chest and between the shoulders. The putter blade has not changed from its address angle because the dimple of the left arm is held looking upward to prevent any roll (or further supination) of the arm, and both hands are arched.

Maybe two days of putting on the hall carpet is enough for you to feel the difference between Hogan's system and your "handsy process." Perhaps you can soon hit the sweet spot nine out of ten times because you let the magical device, and not your hands, steer the club's head. The tempo feels good—even hovering is beginning to feel better. You may have even experimented with the lower left hand grip and found it works very well—as long as the palms of your hands face each other with thumbs down the shaft pointing to the ball. It is interesting to note that both Arnold Palmer and Gary Player, interviewed separately, provided the same answer to the question: "If you had your wonderful careers to do all over again . . . would you do anything different?"

Their immediate answer: "Yes, I think I would have tried the low left hand grip for putting."

I asked Mr. Palmer why . . . and he said, "In order to keep that left hand from breaking down."

He wrote an admonishment in his 1960s book, *The Arnold Palmer Method*:

HOMEWORK

Put a dime down on the rug, then step away six feet, and drop a ball. Once again, line yourself up to the target line, check your connection points, then hover the blade. When you arch both hands toward the ball, you will feel a nice squeeze on the last three fingers of the left hand (apologies to the lefties—lead hand). If you are too tense, then the clubhead will jump around. A simple way to relax is to make certain both knees are slightly flexed all the way through the stroke.

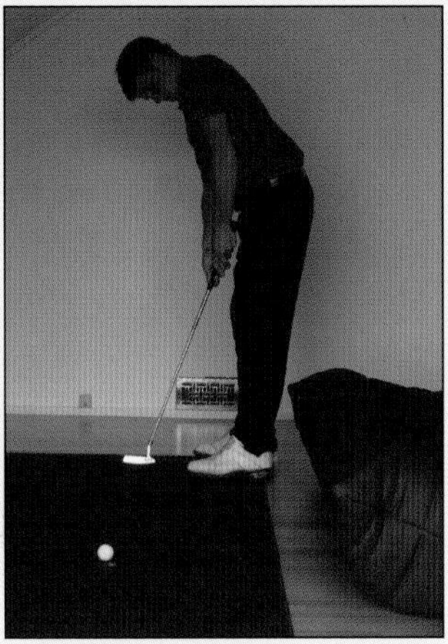

Putting to a dime.

Now, take a mental photo of the dime—and tilt the triangle with a slow push down of the left shoulder.

The back of the left hand should be angled toward the ground if you have not moved your hands. Remember—let the tilt of the triangle move the hands into the proper position. Just like the mirror drill, the hands do not move independently.

Your last thought is of the dime target, and perhaps you are close enough to see it in your peripheral vision. You can imagine the target line. That's good, just keep the target in your mind's eye even though you are looking with your "dominant eye" to a spot on the back of the ball that you are going to kiss with the sweet spot marked on your putter blade.

"Keep the left hand ahead of the ball."

And that's exactly what Hogan's Magical Device will do for you.

By now, if you are stroking through the ball confidently with a solid feel in your arched hands, perhaps it is time to take it outside. But I would like you to stay away from the holes on the practice green . . . go to the edge, away from distractions, and put a tee in the ground. Then you're ready for your thirty daily putts from six feet. It really is poor and mostly negative learning to putt to a cup, because you must admit, you sink only about fifteen percent. Putt to a tee peg. Remember that "pace is more important than line" anyway. Besides, you're just learning a new technique—so please play along with these temporary rules for the rest of your seven-day commitment.

PHOTO CREDIT: Burrard International

Jack Nicklaus in a crouch such as Hogan adopted later in an attempt to get closer to the ball. Nicklaus is still using the triangle to control the path of the clubface through the ball. Left shoulder up . . . ball in the cup.

One day soon, when you get back to putting "one ball, at one hole" you can imagine your tee peg stuck into the edge of the hole in exactly the place over which you would want the ball to roll in order to knock the tee and ball into the hole. This toppling tee is a great vision for your next real putt out on the course. And you will develop this visualization from your putting drill of thirty six-footers at a tee peg.

When you have a golfing match, the final thing you should do before going to the first tee is stroke five or six putts to a tee peg—just four-footers that bounce off the tee—and short putts won't bother you all day.

Your next step, when you get very good at six-footers, is to place two tees twenty feet apart and putt one ball back and forth. When you start getting pretty consistent, and pretty confident, maybe it's time to take this out onto the course. Left shoulder up, ball in the cup. If you need a refresher in the middle of a game, remember these USGA rules:

- Rule 7-1b: "Practice putting or chipping on or near the first teeing ground before starting a round or play-off is permitted."
- Rule 7-2: "A player must not make a practice stroke during play of a hole. Between the play of two holes, a player must not make a practice stroke, except that he may practice putting or chipping on or near:
  - the putting green of the hole last played.

PHOTO CREDIT: Mike Lilly

Jim Furyk, 2010 Phoenix Open Champion, practicing his putting with the lower left hand grip at Thousand Oaks, California.

- any practice putting green.
- the teeing ground of the next hole to be played in the round.

Vijay Singh takes advantage of these rules during slow play. On the tee he putts or chips to the thin leg of a bench. Just five-footers, mainly for feel of the sweet spot. The surface doesn't really matter, as you may have concluded from doing the six-foot putting drill around your house at a dime. You can tell when you've hit the ball solid—on the sweet spot—with your clubface square to the target.

Ben Crenshaw—one of the great putters on the tour, respected for his two Masters victories in 1984 and 1995 as well as being U.S. Ryder Cup captain in 1999—emphasized that one should not try to look like someone else while putting. You should be yourself, but there was no doubt that certain rules are used by every good putter. We were on the plane from Pebble Beach to San Francisco, and as a Hogan historian, he praised the great man's credo: "Pace is more important than line." He was not sure, however, about Hogan's recommendation of a strong grip. Crenshaw did not like the idea of anyone being "too tight" to the point of tension. There had to be feel in the shot, but a grip had to be worked on by the individual, because the hands must not break down. Therefore, hovering was good.

The care Hogan had to take with the dangerous greens set for a major golf tournament is expressed by a note from an anonymous pro to his friend:

PHOTO CREDIT: Mike Lilly

Tiger warming up with short putts to a dime before a round.

"I was 2 feet off the putting surface in 2 inch rough on the fringe of the green and had a tricky and slippery chip down to the hole which was in the middle of the green. I hit a perfect chip shot which made its way to the hole but forgot to stop and it rode the massive false front slope of the green and rolled all the way thru the green and ended up 25 yards in the fairway."
— *Morais's Golf Adventures*

The photo on the following page was taken at Winged Foot Golf Club in Mamaroneck, New York, during the 1959 U.S. Open. Hogan, with his eye problem, tied for eighth place following a "disastrous" seventy-six on his final round on Sunday.

You can see that for a putting stroke, there are dozens of details to be ingrained—you can't remember them all and then select them from the left side of your brain as you try to make a golf shot. These details have to be incorporated into the right brain—the more visual side—and become a reactive part of a process that becomes feel and habit to you. May I remind you gently . . . it takes only one week of hitting thirty putts during the day to a dime or a tee peg—and you are a significantly better putter. Can you believe there are those who don't have the patience for even that small a chore?

LONG PUTTS WITH BEN HOGAN'S SYSTEM

Make no mistake, Ben Hogan was not just a good putter, he was a great putter, even though he downplayed his own abilities due to the frustration he felt after the near death car accident in 1949.

A negative reputation concerning his putting ability began following that horrific automobile crash which cut his left eye and ruined his depth perception. After he resumed his career, often reaching lofty heights, he began to take a longer and longer time over the putt. When asked, following his victory at the Western Open, why he had stood for so long over the putt on the final hole, his answer was characteristically short: "Because I couldn't see it going in yet." This defensive answer perhaps foreshadowed the creeping loss of his sight. But still, there were

PHOTO CREDIT: Getty Images

Hogan on the treacherous greens of Winged Foot during the 1959 U.S. Open in the lower crouch he changed to as his sight degenerated. He also knew that on very fast greens, choking down lowered the putter's swing weight for more feel. This one missed but he's still left with a gimme.

brilliant moments: In the wonderful book by Mark Frost titled simply *The Match*, Hogan is one up on the eighteenth hole at Cypress Point—a course that Hogan loved, and which Jack Nicklaus calls the Sistine Chapel of golf—in a preparation match before the Bing Crosby National Pro-Am in 1956. It was supposed to be a private match on one of the three courses of the Crosby tournament—the other two being Pebble Beach and Spyglass Hill—all three scenic, world class challenges.

The match began with perhaps fifty spectators as Ben Hogan and partner Byron Nelson, two famous and iconic professionals, faced two amateurs: Ken Venturi

HOME DRILL

Complete thirty repetitions of six-foot putts every day for seven days.

Before you try to put this putting system into your game, give it a week of practice with about thirty or forty balls a day. Find a piece of carpet in the basement—throw a dime on the floor and putt over it. Get used to the fluid and relaxed stroke when the clubhead is not grounded. Just tilt the Magical Device for seven days in a row, anywhere you can get it done and whenever.

This putting drill is just a way to introduce you to a system—step by step, rather than burying you with a great many details at once. If you get bored, you can move on to apply this same putting stroke to short, ten-foot chips. Ingrain the feel of strong hands by powering and stabilizing the stroke with the Magical Device. Then get ready to move on through longer putts, to chips, then lobs, and half shots.

For a long putt, the stance is wider for stability. The right elbow is still connected to the waist area, although the right elbow but may be pulled off the crest of the pelvis and across the abdomen on a long follow-through. Only the triangle moves, tilted by the left shoulder going straight up to the sky—not pulled away from the target line. The right knee releases under the ball so that the hands can remain in the Hogan mold in front of the chest without breaking down.

and Harvie Ward, both with stellar amateur records but two leading golfers who preferred to keep their amateur status along the image of the quintessential amateur, Robert Tyre Jones. (Venturi eventually relented, and won the 1964 U.S. Open as a professional on Maryland's Congressional Country Club Blue course.)

Word of this spectacular match spread quickly, and by the tenth hole there were an estimated five thousand hushed fans watching as Ben Hogan hit three perfect shots on the uphill, par five tenth to go one up with a brilliant eagle.

From there on, the beautiful course wound out of the hills and pine trees down among sand dunes and wild grass toward the ocean cliffs. The four determined competitors halved every hole with birdies past the oceanside fifteenth hole.

The sixteenth, arguably the loveliest par three in the world—and announced by its handicap position as the third most difficult hole of the eighteen—was halved again. The hole was cut to the back so that the distance from the back tee was over 240 yards through the ocean mist. The green was like a round head on a thin neck, and cliffs pounded by surf flanked it on both sides. Hogan took driver and with his classic power fade avoided the beach on the left and found the green for his par. Nelson and Ward birdied for another half. Ben and Byron remained one up.

Because of its isolation, the seventeenth hole at Cypress is probably one of the better, albeit lesser-known, holes in golf's great array of gorgeous settings. From the sixteenth green, the golfers climb a granite hill covered with a low tangle of ice plant and hardy grass to a tee on a promontory jutting like a fist into the Pacific Ocean. If you could see that far, you'd be looking at Japan.

Back toward the mainland lies a straightaway manicured fairway beckoning the golfer to aim to the left of a dense grove of escape-proof cypress trees which block any "ordinary" shot from a view of the green. The left side demands a long, straight drive of at least 280 yards for the four hundred yard dogleg. To the right of the trees lies a narrow track of grass beside the cliffs just wide enough for a maintenance truck. Hogan selected his one iron, and with a power fade, dropped the ball six feet from the cliff's edge, with an eight iron left to the oceanside green. So certain was he of his accuracy, he spun the ball away from the trees toward the cliff's edge. Hogan and Nelson held on to their tenuous one stroke lead.

When Ken Venturi holed a birdie on the final sloping green by the white clubhouse, he threatened to tie Hogan and his partner Byron Nelson. Hogan stepped confidently up to a slippery nine footer on greens stimping at twelve, and ran his birdie putt home with a smile and a promise: "I don't lose to amateurs."

Venturi and Ward had a better ball total of fifty-nine. Hogan shot a sixty-three, tying his own course record, and Nelson had a sixty-seven. Their better ball was fifty-eight—fourteen under par.

For further proof of his putting ability, we must remember with respect, that Hogan won nine major tournaments—ten by Hogan's count which included the Hale American Open in 1942. Helen Ross, PGA Tour chief of correspondents, explains: "The 1942 open was labeled the 'wartime' U.S. Open at Ridgemoor in Chicago, with the USGA involved but not sponsoring the event, and thus not recognizing it as an official Open. Still Hogan didn't take this championship—named the Hale American National Open—any less seriously. His sixty-two in the second round is still the lowest ever shot in a 'U.S. Open.' No wonder Hogan steadfastly claimed he won five U.S. Opens."

However, his official nine major wins puts Hogan fourth, behind only Jack Nicklaus with eighteen, Tiger Woods with fourteen, and Walter Hagen with eleven. Although those wins occurred while putting on

The magnificent sixteenth (par three) at Cypress Point through a winter mist.

The isolated seventeenth tee at Cypress Point where the golfer must choose the route. The main fairway left of the cypress grove is long; the small path to the right is dangerous. Hogan hit a one iron fade down the edge of the trees to the cliff's edge, followed by an eight iron to the green.

unusually fast and tricky greens, Hogan was able to play in heated competition without a three putt for four full, pressure-packed rounds. These remarkable performances were due to his system—and his strategy: Where do I want the ball to be if it misses the hole?

For long putts, take a wide stance for stability, with much of your weight on the inside of the right shoe. Because your right elbow is at your waist, your left shoulder is higher than the right. This position allows you to glance down the target line easily, and you will immediately see that it offers you a clear view to the hole. When you take a picture of that scene with your mind's camera, you don't have to think about distance—just let the whole scene sink into the right side of your brain and stroke toward that memory by tilting the triangle.

You'll know if you kept your head still—as you think of the image in your mind—because as you stroke the ball away, you will see a "halo" outline on the spot where it used to be. (It's called eidetic imagery I seem to remember from Psych 101.)

You are not expecting long putts to roll in—although

This was the shortcut Hogan chose for his drive at the seventeenth at Cypress.

some will. Hogan's main objective was to put the ball into gimme range for a certain two putt. "Putt to a manhole cover," was his instruction, just as he did at Carnoustie for the British Open title in 1953. At the par five sixth hole, 570 yards in length, he had four two-putt birdies for the four rounds of the Open to win with a six under par total on the 7,368 yard ordeal called "The Beast." Of course his long play strategy was pretty good too. He always considered where the best place strategically would be for the ball to wind up. He did this especially on treacherous PGA Tour greens—if the first putt missed, where would the best place be for it to finish within gimme range? Also, the first putt would never finish above the hole when it would call for a slippery downhill putt for the par. An uphill putt was always his choice.

When approaching a green with the pin on the left side, Hogan would aim at the center of the green and "work" the approach iron's flight from the center toward the pin—the same formula would be used for a far right pin. Hogan did this religiously, earning Lee Trevino's praise and reflection: "Is there anything really wrong with putting from the center of the green?"

Roll is so important for long putts and it is easier to develop the target seeking top-spin roll if you catch the ball on the upswing of the club's arc.

With the weight on your right foot you know that the bottom of the club's arc will be well back down the target line from the ball when you place the ball just inside the left heel. With the club hovering at address, the ball will be struck with a rising clubhead pulled up by the left shoulder. What a feeling . . . as the club's sweet spot hits the center of the ball just below the equator. Instant forward roll, and a putt that gives you perfect weight.

For long putts there is a tendency to lessen the arch of the left hand and a "pull" may result. Remember that this "twist and arch" grip provides a stable and reliable contact with the ball—where the putter blade doesn't open or close the slightest bit—because the hands don't move.

A further caution for long putts is to tilt the triangle through impact with the ball, completely, so that there is never a "hit and stop." You are not using your lower body yet, but for really long putts, a golfer has to give release to the upper body as the left shoulder reaches its highest point. The left shoulder is still parallel to the target line, but has to go somewhere . . . so before it pulls to the left away from the target line, the right heel lifts a bit and pushes the right knee a few inches

On a slippery green Hogan wanted to leave an uphill sure thing if the first putt stayed out.

toward the target. It pushes against a firm but flexed left knee and the inside edge of the left shoe. Both elbows are still connected firmly to the rib cage. The hands are past impact by now, and are pushed down the target line between the shoulders. The effect is that the hands remain in their mold—and in their position between the shoulders. Both hands hold their position, and point down the line toward the target. The chest is turning toward the target but never quite gets "full on" unless you fully release the lower body, which sometimes happens—such as on Jack Nicklaus's famous putt in 1986 at Augusta's seventeenth hole. His left hand separated from the right, and the left arm went on straight up in a triumphant salute to the birdie which would take him to his sixth Masters championship at age forty-six. It is interesting to see in the picture that although Jack was striding after the ball, the left hand never lost its commanding control of the club.

Another point to be aired when discussing putting is posture. Fatigue or concentration sometimes causes the shoulders to hunch over, and the head droops to the point where a clean and smooth takeaway and swing through the ball is not to be achieved. Fatigue affecting posture over the last seven or eight holes can ruin a promising game. So, just as a golfer must go through a countdown for proper alignment, he should also remind himself of the need to push the shoulders back with the neck aligned to a straight spine and not drooping down until the chin is almost on the chest.

Following his left eye injury, the frustration over putting that Hogan lived with is shown by his cryptic observance: "There is no similarity between golf and putting; they are two different games, one played in the air, and the other on the ground." However, as you read more from this book, you will see that the takeaway and impact positions for the putt and short chip are miniatures of a full shot's impact zone.

For over-spin, the swing arc should rise from below the equator on the ball. Hover the putter behind the ball knowing that the clubhead's arc will be at the lowest point opposite the foot bearing the most weight.

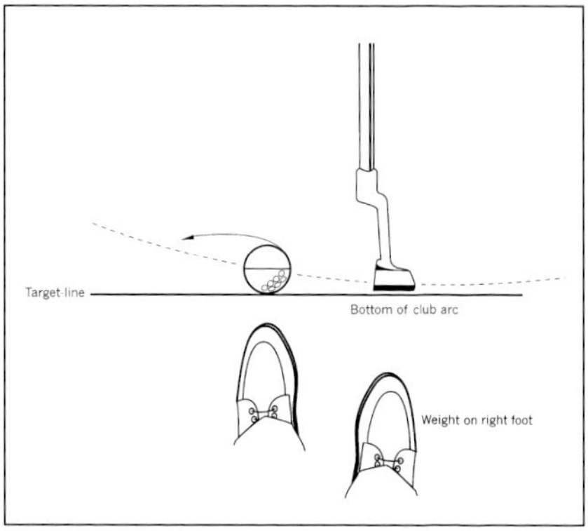

Later in life, as age emphasized Hogan's visual frustrations, the great champion would play golf with his fellow members at the Colonial Club in West Texas, but upon arriving at the green he would pick up his ball and pocket it.

In one case, the members were determined to test themselves against one of the game's greatest legends, and thus contrived a game where Mr. Hogan would play the ball from tee to green, and his caddy would putt out. Money was bet on the sly, because Hogan had warned, "If there's money involved, I don't want to hear about it." The match began with several dozen members following along, watching to see if the best ball from three members could beat Hogan's "assisted" score.

The chosen caddy was "Big Harry" Cotter, who knew Hogan from Quail Creek Golf Club in Oklahoma. Harry's dad was part owner, and Hogan liked to stop by when in the neighborhood. Big Harry played football for the Oklahoma Sooners, was to serve in the Marines in Vietnam, and was a scratch golfer in his own right.

The big-money match is best described by the caddy himself in complete detail, and with appropriately accented dialogue: "From the first tee, par four, 390 yards, Mr. Hogan faded a drive to the right side of center, then he hit

Did Phil Mickelson refer to Hogan for a long putt stance? With weight on the back foot the swing arc will be rising into the ball for lots of roll.

Model in Hogan pose with head behind the ball where it is easy to peer down the line to the cup.

a pitching wedge three feet; I made the putt—birdie—one up. On the next hole, par four, 428 yards, Mr. Hogan faded a drive 250 yards then skipped a five iron in eight feet. I sank the putt for a birdie—two up."

The show continued through the ninth and final hole; Big Harry had ridden Mr. Hogan's immaculate shot-making for a twenty-nine with his own wagers totaling just under $3,000. "Mr. Hogan hit nine greens inside fifteen feet—I sank seven of them . . . and that was enough for the members."

Assessing the great man, the caddy said in reflection: "It was very tough to get Mr. Hogan to play members because he was not a real friendly guy. If he liked you, he'd do anything for you. People thought he was rude, but he just wanted to play golf—not to visit."

There has been a lot to remember so far, but here is one more point that might become your favorite, last swing thought before you putt or chip to the image of the pathway into the hole: Be aware of the highest point for the tip of the left shoulder while at address, because after the takeaway—when you raise your left shoulder to bring the club back to the ball—your right shoulder must pass "under" that high spot. Get into the habit, because it will be the same for all shots from putter to driver . . . and one day you might thank me for this nuance.

CHAPTER 3

CHIPPING WITH HOGAN'S MAGICAL DEVICE

THE NICKLAUS VIEWPOINT

Jack Nicklaus has said that the first short move away from the ball is the most important of the entire swing . . . that it is also the easiest to do . . . but hardly anyone does it properly. Golfers put the clubhead on the ground for a feeling of security, then flick it away from the ball—either inside the target line or to the outside; either track will send the chip off line. If the golfer learns to hover the clubhead, as so many do, (just the way you would in the sand trap) one quickly discovers whether your arms are too tight or not, because the clubhead will jump around if you are tense. A firm squeeze of the last three fingers of the left hand and the first two of the right hand will bring back a familiar feeling of relaxed strength and the molded grip which, when arched, will never break down.

Hogan hovered the clubhead an inch or more behind the ball and moved the hands away from the ball a foot or two with a rhythmical push of the left shoulder, without any movement of his lower body. This start assured a smooth takeaway without stubbing the grass, or moving the lower body. In this way the

Note that the takeaway for a short chip is really the putting action. The back of the left hand is angled toward the ground because the hands have not rotated on their own. The triangle tilts. The lower body does not move.

swing began with a slow tempo which did not hit its highest speed until coming back through the impact zone. So, the takeaway began both the full swing and putt with the same effective smooth and relaxed tempo, and on a track parallel to the target line with nothing rushed, or fearful, or out of alignment: "The most important part of the swing" . . . maybe somebody should do it correctly. Unfortunately, this first stage is probably the first one to be forgotten, and you'll wonder why you're skying the ball or coming over the top again.

Later, you will find how Hogan confused a lot of folks who thought that his waggle was the same action as his takeaway—which it wasn't. The first stage of the takeaway uses a shoulder tilt to move the hands. The waggle is all hands as a pre-swing practice of Hogan's secret left-hand move as you will see in Chapter Five.

SHORT CHIPS

Take your six iron and chip thirty balls from just off the practice green ten to twenty feet from the cup, with hands held firmly in the arched position and thumbs pointing down at the ball. For this shot, adopt as much of the putting drill as possible before we move on to longer shots which will involve lower body movement. For this chipping drill, keep the lower body out of the shot—the main objective here is in getting the feel of your triangle and the connection to the big muscle groups of the torso. So assume a good foundation with your weight on the front foot and the ball aligned with the left heel. Why? Because if you don't move below the waist, the bottom of the arc for the clubhead will be right on the ball and will not change.

Play the shot like a putt, with your six or seven iron from just off the green. Let the ball land just on the green for it to run to the target like a putt. Don't be surprised if it goes in.

At address the ball is positioned just inside the left heel. Knees slightly flexed. The model's toe line is in a closed position in order to better feel the action of the right shoulder coming under the ball from the infield, rather than over the top—a flaw which is more likely to creep into the swing with an open stance, along with the tendency to open the hips as well. For now, please practice with the left foot in the closed position closer to the target line than the right.

If you find that on contact, your ball does not make a click sound when struck, it is possible that you do not have your elbows strongly connected to the rib cage, or that you have tried to hit the ball with the hands. Move the triangle and hit with molded hands.

You will very quickly gain confidence about the reliability and steadiness of this upper body shot, which is powered by the triangle—Hogan's Magical Device. With the same smooth takeaway and a hovering club, the chips are now starting to hit the target regularly, and are just about all within gimme range. As with a long putt, where you don't use any body release, you may feel the right elbow pull off the crest of the pelvis and drag along the torso toward your belt buckle, but the shoulders remain parallel to the target line until the hips arrive at a point where they must be released by raising the right heel.

Here is another extremely effective nuance of Hogan's Magical Device for chipping. The elbow dimples are held pointing upward toward the sky,

Hover the club an inch behind the ball before the left shoulder pushes down for the takeaway. The hands do not move by themselves. Push down with the left shoulder to tilt the triangle. The hands ride the triangle so that the back of the left hand is angled to the ground behind the ball.

and the impact position is assumed at address—closed stance, weight shifted left, and with just a short takeaway controlled by the left shoulder. The subtlety lies with the left arm, which is held in the position of elbow dimple to the sky (or supination) so that the clubface does not roll closed from its square position.

For the downswing, raise the left shoulder which tilts the triangle, and the club returns to the ball for the chip onto the green. The lower body is steady as for putting. The firm structure of the hands provides plenty of force to the ball as the triangle swings through so that there is no need for a "hit" from the hands.

The impact position for the hands is maintained throughout the chip, which has the effect of the back of the arched left hand facing down at the back of the ball—just like a long putt.

As the short chips lengthen into pitches, lobs, and half-swing shots, the lower body is brought into play in a special way, as we shall soon see. But with short chips, you bring the Magical Device back through the ball by raising the left shoulder. This gives you a solid feel because of the arched hand position, and the stability provided by the torso connected to the arms by pressure at the armpits, as well as the right elbow attached to the crest of the pelvis.

Don't let the hands move independently. The connected triangle moves them through the ball over steady, flexed knees. And don't lose the arch and twist position of both hands. (The change in hand action will come in the next section.)

If the chipping action for short shots is not immediately absorbed, don't panic. Keep putting, and keep chipping this way for a few more sessions until the action feels comfortable and reliable. Repeating this feeling is important; some might try to memorize these instructions instead of experiencing them, but they'll miss out. Ten or fifteen short chips down the hall carpet at home is a good way to keep in touch with all parts of the process. The repeated click of the ball on the sweet spot will tell you of your progress. The occasional clack sound, or feeling of looseness, will signal the breakdown of the left hand when it makes contact with the ball. But you now

Chipping down the hall to the staircase is a quick and easy way to review all of the details of your chipping stroke.

know what to do: Hold the arch of the hands and don't move them. Squeeze the last three fingers of the left hand as you arch.

In his book, Hogan encouraged golfers to "practice his drills fifteen minutes per day for one week." This prescription is surprisingly close to laboratory research, which states, "For an action to be absorbed into a reflex response, the action should be repeated forty to fifty times per day in conscious repetition—for seven days." By then, it should have been programmed as a memory, to operate as a reflex, leaving you to think only about the target to which the ball will run.

When the chipping action of the magical device has been absorbed, it's time to build on the same action for pitches and lobs.

If by this time you are still apprehensive about the wisdom of trying Hogan's idea for one week, read this opinion from George Knudson—a Hogan disciple with one of the truly great swings. Knudson won twenty-five professional tournaments—eight on the PGA Tour—and tied for second place in the 1969 Masters. He met Hogan, his idol, in two unflattering situations. The first was when he jumped over a fence at Augusta to watch Hogan practice. The other when he met Hogan at the club in Fort Worth. Knudson sauntered in wearing blue jeans and an afro. Hogan sent him away to "dress

Note the flexed left knee toward which the right knee will begin to move. The chest begins to turn down the target line with hands in their firm grip in front.

like a professional" and, so great was his respect for "Bantam Ben," Knudson came back with a haircut and grey slacks with a navy blue jacket, then cooly offered Hogan a Canadian cigarette. Hogan looked him up and down and said, "If they're as smooth as your swing, I think I will." A friendship began.

In his book, *The Natural Golf Swing*, Knudson was on point with Hogan's repeating action when he observed: "We don't hit at the ball, rather, we swing a unit—our hands, arms, and club—indeed, our whole body, through the ball toward our target. We focus on the target. The ball simply gets in the way of the clubhead . . . ."

Knudson then challenges every serious golfer to find the swing motion during which he is in balance and in a posture which will bring the clubhead to the ball consistently.

Wouldn't you consider such a swing? It begins with the shoulder tilt and hand position you learned when putting and chipping. Hogan believed that the impact action for a putt and chip were miniature versions of the impact zone for the full shot.

Using this molded and powerful hand position, putts and chips are powered by the gentle tilt of the shoulders. There is never a handsy or loose pass at the ball. Simply put, for Hogan and his protégés Leonard and Knudson, the ball seems to get in the way of that solid structure driven by a slow-moving and controlling left shoulder.

Here is the strong hand position controlled by tilting shoulders which bring the clubface back to the ball with structural strength. This dramatic image illustrates the arched palmar flexion described by golfing savant Moe Norman as "twist and arch." For putting and chipping with this unyielding structure the thumbs point to the ball.

CHAPTER 4

THE PITCH SHOT

When Hogan's solid hand structure is learned, felt, and practiced (through putting and chipping) so that solid "on-the-button" contact with the ball is common, it is time to move up a level to the very important pitch shot—the shot needed when you are twenty to forty yards from the pin with not much in your way and you have to get it close. Because of the longer distance, the pitch shot will require important changes to the swing as you take the club away to waist high. So go to the short game area, and practice twenty pitch shots to different targets. The left knee moves in toward the stationary right knee—not toward the target line—when the club gets back to the point where the build up of tension forces the need for a release before the right hip can sway away from the target. That right knee must remain steady, with weight on the inside edge of the shoe—like the inside edge of a ski or skate—so the slight bending of the left knee towards the stationary right knee releases this tension. The right hip rotates clockwise back toward the target over a stable right knee, and the wrists begin to hinge into dorsiflexion.

Then, on the downswing to impact, when the left shoulder tilts upwards, the right knee moves with the right hip through contact. Just a slow connected action through the ball.

Hogan holds the strong connection with elbows on the rib cage to use his torso to power an accurate pitch shot to the green where it will roll toward the pin.

A good way to get the feel for Hogan's system is to stay in a closed stance for chips and pitches. The closed stance prepares you for the faster and more complicated longer shots to come, and gets you into the habit of the right side "coming under the ball" down the "infield path" and not "over the top." However, I don't know what level you are; perhaps you open your stance for short and medium shots. The main focus is the hand-set for impact—no matter what ball position you use. Hogan wanted his golf ball opposite his left heel.

Let's watch a mild-mannered surgeon—who doesn't have much time for practice—use Hogan's technique to click that ball to the center of the green. He can repeat this shot in the rec room of his basement and up the carpeted stairs.

The golfer model in this sequence is very keen on stolen practice time, however short. Like Hogan, whenever and wherever he can review the system is a vacation for the mind. Psychology tells us that if a golfer has a system then specific practice as above is akin to shooting hoops. There is an attention to the immediate result when hitting a golf ball, so even just a very few shots are valuable. Not to be too far-fetched about the effect of focused practice, but studies have demonstrated that experimental groups imagining the action of a skill do significantly

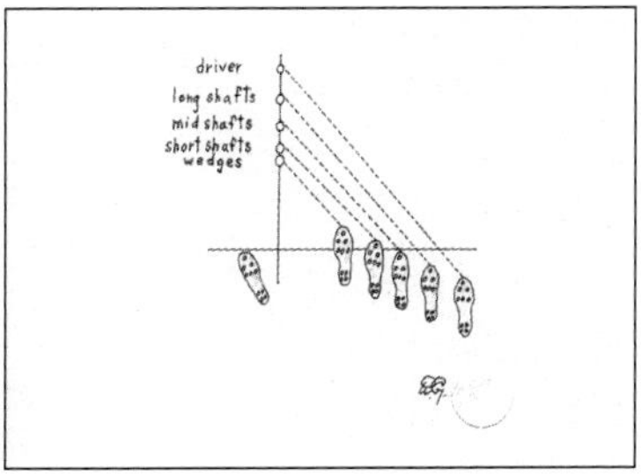

The foot positions Hogan recommended positioned the ball off the inside left heel for almost all normal shots. He knew some pros moved the ball across the stance, but was convinced that it was better to get used to one position for the ball in relation to the inside of his left heel.

At address the model holds a strong connection with elbows on the rib cage. The stance is "closed" but the stance lines are parallel to the target line like "railroad tracks."

The shaft at this stage should be parallel to the target line with the wrists ready to hinge into dorsiflexion. The left knee moves inward.

better than subjects who do nothing; and those in the imagination group are not too far behind subjects who do the actual practice—so there is nothing wrong with five or six putts to a dime on the carpet while reviewing Hogan's system.

An even faster "practice" session would be merely to imagine and mimic the images such as these below.

At impact the right knee moves under the ball with the first upward movement of the left shoulder. The right shoulder turns under the address point of the left shoulder at address.

The right side releases under the ball to the finish where one can see that the hands have not changed from their address position.

The golfer takes the relaxed finish down from the follow-through which is a natural reaction to the hands maintaining their mold—just as Hogan, Knudson, and Norman did.

« A beneficial swing thought is the image of a strong rubber band attached to the right knee from the shoulder. The golfer should be aware of the left shoulder at address and make sure that the tip of the right shoulder moves under the highest point of the left shoulder on the way to impact the ball.

As the left shoulder rises the right knee drives under the ball into impact. »

The left shoulder continues to rise and signals the entire right side to release through the ball. Distance to the shot is increased in relation to the speed of the right side releasing through the impact zone. Later on we will focus on this timing.

Avoid traffic and time spent on excess organization by using your office, backyard, or hallway to accommodate a short daily visit with the elusive coordination of the golf swing. It keeps you in touch; and it clears your mind as well.

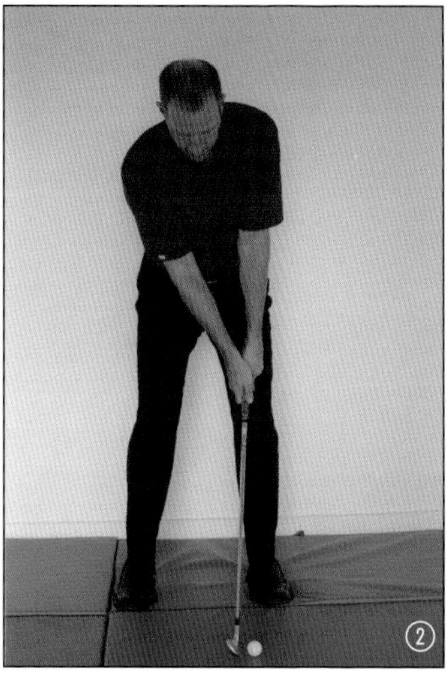

Find a place at home to work your memory bank with three of the stages for short chips.

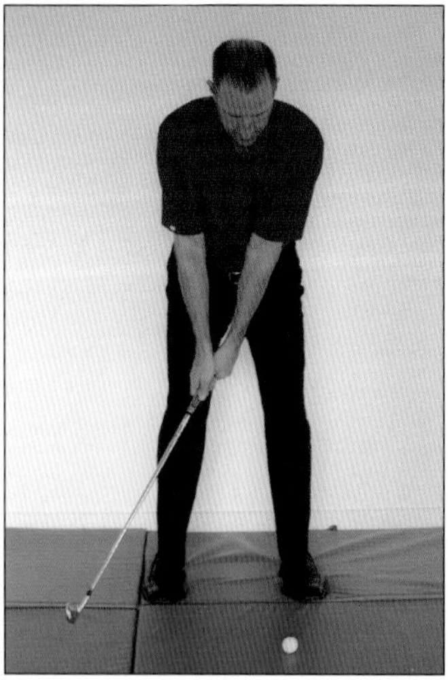

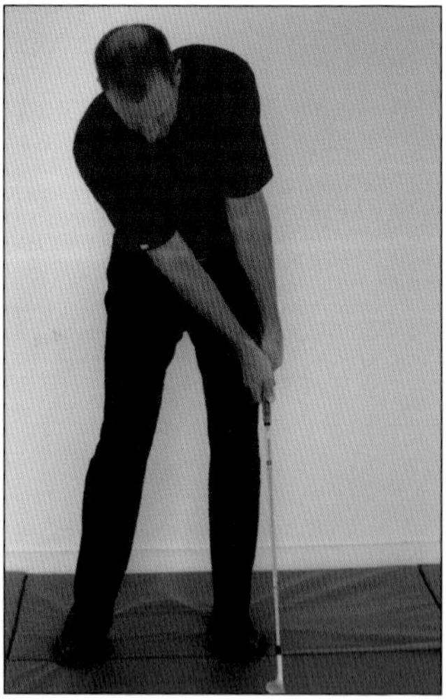

CHAPTER 5

THE HALF SHOT FOR ACCURACY WITH HOGAN'S "SECRET"

From fifty to one hundred yards out and wanting to get close for a birdie putt, check your connection points and turn away from the target with a good image of where you want to land this shot. There is nothing wrong with the center of the green.

The takeaway brings your hands higher than the waist, but you are in a position of strength because both elbows are still connected to the rib cage and guided by the Magical Device. At the top, both hands are in dorsiflexion ready for the move into the impact zone.

Now that you have practiced the Magical Device there is an understanding by the feel that it is a strong way the shoulders, arms, and torso are connected for power and accuracy. It is at this juncture we introduce Hogan's Secret, which you will see is the hand action used for impact which accelerates the power stored for striking the ball like no other attempt at acceleration can. An arm-swing speed-up can't come close, and this fact goes unexamined by many amateurs—especially

Hogan has turned his chest over a firm right knee to the top of the backswing for the half shot. His right elbow is still connected to the hip area. Both hands are in dorsiflexion

women. A faster leg drive can get things like one's clubhead arc, and club-shaft plane out of control. Hogan's secret is highly effective in keeping control because it is an isolated action, set in the center of a solid torso driven foundation. Further, considering the sometimes violent moves by the body, the left hand action is short and minor. This move has been the "self-discovered" tool that touring pros kept from amateurs for fifty-five years that I know about. You're going to love it.

APPLYING HOGAN'S SECRET AT IMPACT: THE KEYSTONE TO A COMPETITIVE GOLF SWING

Specifically, the "secret" is the way the left hand is twisted from dorsiflexion on the way down into an arched position at impact. This hand motion is neither "supination" nor "pronation" as people were led to believe during the explanations of more than fifty years ago. It is a squeeze of the last three fingers of the left hand with a simultaneous twist—called palmar flexion—plus an arching of the wrist.

This simple but hidden action by the leading hand was Hogan's secret. So simple, and yet complex enough to hold three important components which, when combined, give you a powerful structure which will not collapse under the stress of impact. This little move will change the way you strike the ball. No doubt you'll like it. Give it a week's trial—it's well worth the time.

a. Squeeze the last three fingers of your leading hand.
b. Twist these fingers into the palm.
c. Simultaneously arch the hand by pointing the long left thumb at the ball.

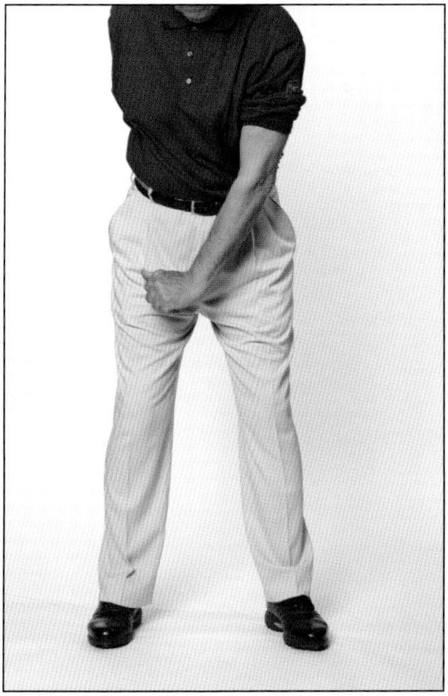

The left hand is still in dorsiflexion.

The leading hand arches and twists with strength as thumb points to ball. The elbow dimple is held pointing to the sky to prevent any "roll over."

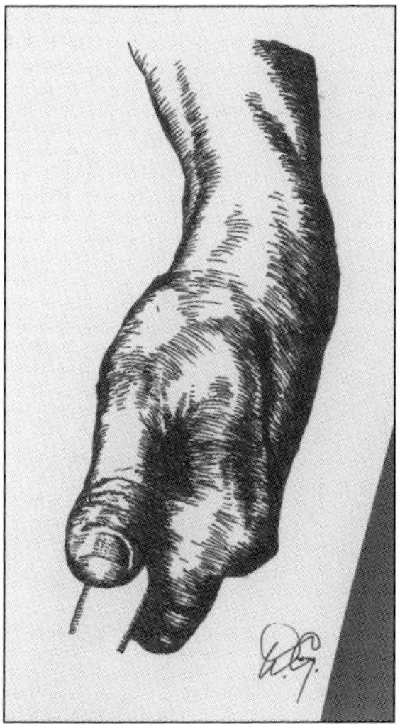

An artist's version of Hogan's left hand at impact. The left arm is held in supination throughout the entire swing, with the inside dimple of the left elbow facing the sky. This rigid position prevents any further rolling of the arm which could pull the ball left of the target. If the twist and arch does not occur, and the left hand rolls over, the ball could be soaring left. Your next inclination would be to "block the release"—and the next one goes right.

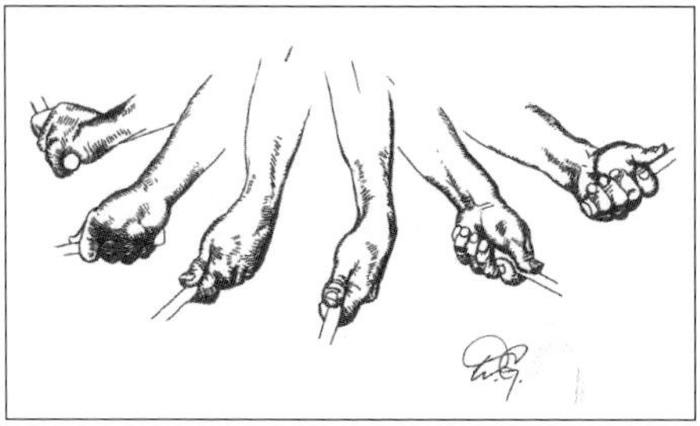

The sequential action of the left arm held in supination while the hand twists and arches.

And so the argument can be made that the centerpiece to Ben Hogan's detailed golf swing comes down to a simple move by one hand in the space of about twelve inches. The arch and twist of the left hand occurs within a split second at speeds of around one hundred miles per hour. Little wonder it took so long to uncover.

This hand position provided Hogan with a powerful structure which would not break down during high speed impact. The ball goes where it reflects from the clubface. With this solid hand structure, the clubface is held on the target line for a significant length of time which enabled Hogan to "knock the pin down."

THE ROLE OF THE RIGHT HAND

The right hand is along for the ride, hanging on with squeezing strength in the last two fingers. The forefinger and thumb are, by comparison, relaxed. Dorsiflexion is maintained with a firm arch throughout the whole swing—just like your mirror exercise from the first chapter.

The right hand does not hit at the ball, but is merely steered into impact by the right elbow connected to the hip, which, as you no doubt will find, actually pushes the forearm and right hand through the ball—just as the surging right foot drives the right knee and hip through impact.

Here the Magical Device is connected to the chest and in complete control of the hands. The triangle's job is to move the clubhead through the ball on the same plane, time and time again—right on the sweet spot. The hands don't move the club—the tilt of the triangle does.

Move the chest through the half shot while concentrating on a mental picture of the target so that your brain calls for the speed required for that distance. There is just a nice click as the hands arch into the ball. Rehearse the whole sequence from the waist-high, takeaway position, down and through the impact zone, to a half follow-through with your chest square to the target.

This described hand action is the essence of good golf. Ben Hogan lived for that moment. Everything else was to prepare for, and set up, that instant when his universe stood still. Moe Norman was more prosaic, calling striking the ball with this hand action "golf's orgasm."

PHOTO CREDIT: Linda Leonard

Stan Leonard shows the force of the magical device turning through the impact zone in dramatic style with firm connection points.

HOME DRILL: Half shot with or without club

This half shot is tightly controlled, and is very effective in getting close to the pin with a bit of practice. Body connection with the club holds the clubface on line. Hogan added to the strength of his grip by "choking down" on the handle a half inch or more. His rationale lay with the oddity of having the smallest finger of the hand wrapped around the largest part of the club's grip. He found no sense in that.

Turn to the top of the backswing for a pitch shot, checking to see that the left arm is waist high and parallel to the target line. The wrists are hinged so that the shaft is beginning to form a right angle with the arm.

As the golfer moves to the barstool position and enters the impact zone, the hands are over the right knee and the secret is to be applied.

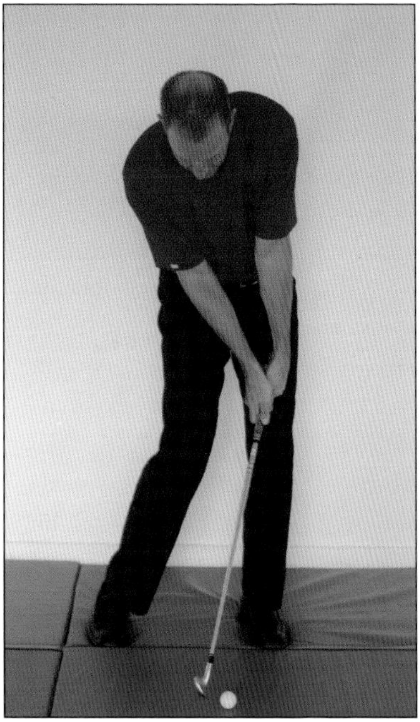

The left shoulder continues to rise so that the hands pass the ball to the left knee as the secret is applied. The hips rotate with speed through the ball.

Hands are held in front of the chest to the half follow-through because of their connection. There is a "mirror effect" with the position of halfway back on the takeaway and the position of halfway on the follow-through. Side-to-side balance, as well as heel-to-toe balance, is necessary for a solid foundation which will guarantee that the bottom of the club's arc, and the path of the club's sweet spot, are both directed at the back of the golf ball.

The beauty of the half shot using Hogan's technique is its accuracy and the strength of hit. It is these two characteristics which come handy in a strong wind when the golfer turns this shot into a "punch shot."

Paul Azinger (or "Zinger" as caddies call him) is very good with the punch shot and I got to watch him as we partnered during his rookie year at Pebble Beach for the Bing Crosby Pro-Am in 1985. Playing in fifty mile per hour gusting winds during a bout of "Crosby Weather," the young Floridian, wearing a short sleeve shirt and a thin pullover, kept complaining about "freezing to death in California."

At the famous seventh hole—a picturesque little par three—it's only 130 yards downhill to a tiny peninsula sticking out into the wind-blown Pacific. The hole is well bunkered, and every so often a creative golfer who wishes to make a point hits a putter down the hill. Not this day. Jim Thorpe, the ex-football player from Morgan State and now a seasoned veteran on the Champions Tour with eighteen wins, had Barry Moss, a switch-hitting outfielder for the Cincinnati Reds, as an amateur partner who went first. Moss aimed at the pin and watched his ball blown sharply left into the ocean, winding up with a triple six. Thorpe adjusted his aim toward the right bunkers but the ball bounded down the hill on the left into the pounding surf for a bogey. Azinger aimed into the wind at the ocean edge of the peninsula to the right, and blew into the left hand bunkers—getting up and down for a par. My turn. Feeling really stupid, I aimed a four iron out into mid ocean from whence it came back to within five feet of the pin for a hard-to-find bird on a difficult day with few highlights.

But back to the punch shot. Hogan advised taking two clubs extra with a half swing and punch down on the back of the ball with strongly connected arms and shoulders. With the weakened left hand grip and the long left thumb, the expected fade will occur. If the wind is from the golfer's right, the wind will hold it straight.

Hogan would maintain the impact position, with his head behind the ball, for as long as possible, and extend the club low after the ball, in order to control the trajectory under the wind.

Punch shot for strength in the wind.

A strong grip and hand structure down and through the ball.

The hands have not left their address position and were moved by the torso's rotation.

For a draw shot, to hold the ball against the wind from the left, take a stronger grip with both hands. A quarter of a turn (forty-five degrees) is normal for most—although Azinger prefers a very strong hand position with a ninety degree turn of the hands. With experimentation you can find your most reliable hand position for a draw that won't bite you in the throat. Hogan called this adjustment "changing the chuck on the lever."

Another move to facilitate a draw is to hold the position of the dimple of the left elbow pointing inward across the front of your chest, and not up to the sky as when you would like a shot with fade action.

Hogan liked to spend a moment or two longer on his right foot to promote the draw. A little experimentation on the practice tee should show your tendencies.

PHOTO CREDIT: Getty Images

A punch shot with perfect balance and a dorsiflexed arched right hand to hold the hands in the classic Hogan mold.

CHAPTER 6

THREE-QUARTER SHOT FOR ACCURACY

The three-quarter shot is a powerful tool when learned. And by studying the connected triangle, learn it you will. When you do catch on, and start hitting the sweet spot eight or nine times out of ten, you can't get enough of it. The feeling of hitting that ball on the money with controlled power is addictive. And this "not-full-out" shot increases your accuracy greatly. Hogan himself changed from an extremely long backswing to the three-quarter swing for greater control in the latter part of his competitive career. He used this swing exclusively during a *Shell's Wonderful World of Golf* episode with Sam Snead and threw a tidy sixty-eight at "the Slammer" for the win. Gene Sarazen, as master of ceremonies, said afterward: "Ben, that was the greatest game of golf I have ever seen. You hit every fairway and every green, and put the ball exactly where you wanted it. Marvelous."

This might be the time to look at Hogan's "plane" for the longer shots. In his famous book *Five Lessons*, Hogan gave a visual presentation for this plane from the address to the top of the shot. It was the image of a golfer taking the club away from the ball to the top of the backswing while under a sheet of glass with

Note that Hogan's right elbow has disconnected from the waist area. Reconnection will be his first priority on the way down to the ball. Hogan's hip line has turned to a full forty-five degrees away from the target line over a stable right knee.

just his head showing through a hole in the window. This posture gave the golfer a solid and balanced position at the top with a controlled relationship to the ball and the target line.

Coming down from the top, however, there was a change. Hogan had his back turned to the target at the top. Then, led by the left knee moving toward the target, he settled onto the barstool. Here, the lower body separates from the upper torso and his hips began to rotate counter-clockwise and away from the target line. His left shoulder had turned toward the target line—and when it rises straight up to sky, the right shoulder turns under this important point.

Hogan spent a lot of time explaining the correct plane—or angle of shoulders to the target line. At the top of the backswing, the golfer turns his shoulders under the glass. This image kept everything parallel to the target line with the butt of the club pointed to the edge of the ball closest to the golfer. However, on the way down, Hogan wanted the plane to change

Take note of the left shoulder at a high point behind the ball. It is under this point that the right shoulder should turn, to avoid any possibility of coming over the top of the ball. The right shoulder and the hands should remain on the "infield" side of the ball through impact with the butt end of the club pointing to the back of the ball.

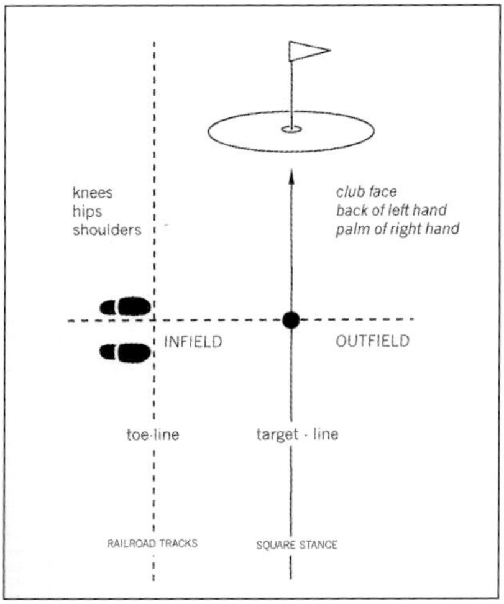

These "railroad tracks" are very important. Alignment to them is given constant attention by competing professionals—sometimes with help from colleagues on the practice tee or on the course from their caddy.

slightly, so that the angle of the shoulders was no longer under the glass pane. In spite of this change, the butt of the club must still point down to the "infield" channel between the golfer's toe line and the ball, because bad things can happen if the hosel moves closer to the ball.

SELF-CHECK LIST

For the mechanical part of the game, golfers can—like an airline pilot—go through a checklist which is best associated with numbers, so that you can make sure you get everything on the list. Then the pilot gets on with flying.

For example, while setting up before you swing at the ball, check:

1. Toe line parallel to the target line.
2. Knees square to target line.

3. Hips square.
4. Shoulders square.
5. Clubface square while hovering.

This check takes only seconds, but is vital for lining up the "railroad tracks." Fatigue or tension tend to get the golfer out of alignment. Check your own position often.

The golfer goes through this alignment process in a second or two then gets on to the main event—the swing—where you are allowed only one swing thought. The best one for the Hogan system is the left shoulder. (Would you believe that someone once wrote an entire book about the role of the left shoulder in the golf swing?) When ready to hit the shot, the golfer must imagine the flight of the ball which includes a picture of the target. You have now departed from the left side of your brain (used for formulae, numbers, and facts) and shifted to the right side of the brain where imagination is king, and you picture your target—perhaps the top of the biggest tree behind the pin—and the ball flight, so that the machinations of the swing are put aside . . . because these details should be ingrained and activated by swing memory like a reflexive action. Swing details should not interfere with the target picture. At least two players—Mac O'Grady and Bob Clampett—have suffered from a bout of "paralysis by analysis." Hogan invented practice, but when he figured out the details, he ingrained them, and always imagined the flight of the ball before striking.

Perhaps this sounds far too complicated. The detailed procedure is just to answer your question of why your shots start to stray for no apparent reason, and to emphasize a common pitfall in golf: Far too many players try to play the game mechanically. Hogan said very clearly: "Hit thirty short putts per day for seven days and you will have the feel for the Magical Device ingrained—then do the same for twenty-foot chips."

When you have ingrained the feel of the controlled tilt of the triangle, and you are playing a match . . . just before you make the shot . . . step away from the ball, take a couple of practice swings and get the memory of the "learned feel" back.

Then step up to the ball, drift into the right side of your brain by looking at the target, focus on the target again, tilt the left shoulder, and feel that memorized snap of Hogan's secret into the ball.

Afterward, analyze the hit to see if you followed your memory bank. If the ball went right, did your left shoulder get past the ball on the takeaway? If the ball went left, did your left shoulder pull away from the target line? If you hit it thin, did you straighten either leg? If you hit it fat, did you sway to the right and move the bottom of the arc away from the back of the ball?

The key is that the checklist should be in your memory bank, and might best be visited with just five or six balls on the practice range before your match . . . when you get Hogan's system as a series of reactions to swing situations, you can hardly wait to get to the ball because it is an inner structure that you can rely on, and follow for each shot automatically. It's like driving a car or shaving. You perform the learned skills without thinking about the details. You know you can make the shot—you have a system. And if you miss . . . you know why. I would strongly suggest that you make sure that you have taken seven days for Chapters Two and Three. You'll feel the use of the connected triangle, and will have taken care of fifty percent of your game. Then take one swing at a time and build to long chip, lobs, half shots, three-quarter shots to the full shot. Focused practice will keep you going through the progression of shots successfully.

PLANE FOR THE THREE-QUARTER SWING

How did Hogan reconnect the right elbow with his hip when he started back down to the impact zone? As the left shoulder is thrust upward, the hands drop into "the slot," and the right elbow drops downward to regain contact with the right waist area. As a result, the left shoulder has not only moved skyward, but also slightly toward the ball on the target line—and there it is: the new shoulder plane that Hogan wanted. This new plane kept him from coming over the top and double-crossing all of his good intentions.

The new plane is encouraged by Hogan's right elbow—bent and touching his right side—so that there is a definite difference in the height of the shoulders and their distance from the target line.

Turning the right shoulder under the highest left shoulder point feels a bit as if the upper body is backing into the ball—until the right shoulder and right side pass under this spot. Corey Pavin practices this and refreshes the feeling while waiting for his turn on the tee.

When this bar stool position (halfway down from the top) is achieved, and you add Hogan's secret—you can hit the ball as hard as you like. From the barstool platform, you can turn your torso through the ball with as much force and speed as you like.

When Hogan said, "I wish I had two right hands to hit it with," it was misleading to a lot of golfers who didn't know that his right hand didn't get out of its dorsiflexion—even when extending down the target line with long shots. He settled into the barstool position and poured on the rotation of his torso. Before this stage, the tempo should be moderate and purposeful.

To consider a possible addition to Hogan's wish for two right hands we might also study the importance of where the butt end of the club is pointing on the way down.

One of the big dangers with pronating the left hand on the takeaway—as many do without realizing it—is that the end of the club's grip points out beyond the ball, to the "outfield" as in the picture on the opposite page. This misdirection—plus an inadvertent slide toward the target—can produce golf's major faux pas: the shank. It's not rocket science to understand that if the hosel of the club moves an inch and a half closer to the ball, you have a "lateral" on your hands.

SHANKING

No one talks about shanking so not many know how to correct it. But all agree that the toughest shot in golf is the one that follows a shank . . . so maybe you should know a little about it.

The butt end of the handle must stay in its own channel down the infield side of the ball, so that contact is made with the center of the club's face. Keeping the hands between the toe line of the golfer's shoes and the target line is the channel to use. Hold the left arm connected to the torso, because disconnection moves the hosel closer to the ball. Disconnection of the right arm encourages an "over the top" move.

If the butt end of the club's grip points to the outfield and the golfer slides the center of his chest past the ball and toward the target, the hosel moves closer to the ball—and the dreaded shank may occur. This model has straightened his right leg on the backswing—a move which is much different from Hogan's stable knee with the weight on the inside edge of the shoe. Too much of a rotation by the hips move the hands too far from the target line to a point "behind" the golfer. The possibility of rotating the hips too far clockwise is greatly reduced by maintaining a stable and flexed right knee. As Hogan said to his caddy: "Know why I'm so goddam good? I never move my knee."

PHOTO CREDIT: Mike Lilly

Sean O'Hair with coach at Sherwood Oaks getting a lesson on alignment during takeaway—a constant subject for study among touring pros. Note the nice extension down the target line with no roll-over of the hands.

PHOTO CREDIT: Mike Lilly

Sean O'Hair at the top of a three-quarter shot with the left shoulder turned behind the ball.

PHOTO CREDIT: Mike Lilly

The attention to setup and alignment requires only seconds and produces a confident setup as Sean O'Hair shows here.

The possibility of a shank brings up another point: Up to now this book has been exaggerating the reach for the ball at address—for the purpose of feeling at address the position of the upcoming impact. Ben Hogan used this trick, and Moe Norman exaggerated it even more for his "position to come back to." But the danger here is reaching out for the ball—and with only an inch or so as the margin for error, the hosel could get in the way and a shank could be the result. So, find the address position for your hands where you are connected and most likely to turn the club's handle down the "infield" making sure you remain in a steady position of balance so that the hands don't "move off" the target. The target is that dimple on the back of the ball where the sweet spot of the club speeds toward the sweet spot within the center of the ball.

One misty morning around 6:00 AM—just after I had shanked nine in a row with a new wedge—Stan Leonard, the Hogan devotee, stated: "You can stand too far from the ball and get burned, because you're reaching for it. But you can't shank from standing too close. Just keep your weight even on the feet. Not on your toes or heels. Posture!"

Then he told me to go away, although not quite in those terms.

Hogan himself fell prey to his own precise system of impacting the ball at the Westchester Classic in 1970 when he surprised three young pros on the first tee with the polite request, "Mind if I join you?" They were at first nervous, then awestruck when Hogan played a fairway wood to within two feet of the pin on the par five twelfth hole for a nice practice round eagle. However, they were shocked into silence on the par three fifteenth when Hogan shanked his ball into a TV tower. Without a change of expression, Hogan took another ball from his taciturn caddy and hit it to the center of the green. No one said a word. With the first ball abandoned, the incident was ignored, dismissed, and forgotten.

The form of this modern player would earn a nod of approval from Hogan. Just look at the attention paid to:

a. The connection at the left shoulder and at the right elbow.
b. The slight arch of the left hand.
c. Flexed knees in an athletic position of readiness.
d. Hovering club head.

Of all the promising young touring professionals like Rory McIlroy and Dustin Johnson, I believe that Mr. Hogan would recognize their talent, and especially the connected torso strength of Ryo Ishikawa who took his Hogan-like swing to the 2010 U.S. Open at Pebble Beach where he finished in 33rd place at eighteen years of age.

CHAPTER 7

THE FULL SHOT WITH THE PITCHING WEDGE

The most important question when arriving at the top of the backswing is often unanswered: What is the move that brings the club handle back down toward the impact zone? Most amateurs avoid the technical answer by merely swinging from the top—a mighty blow as might some angry Scot have taken with a claymore. Hogan's answer was far more effective, even though it had technical demands with a bit of a timing move to master.

Many experts claim that Hogan's first move down from the top happened before his hands got to the horizon—or near to it. With the slow motion cameras running during a PGA broadcast, watch closely and you will see the professional player's hips stop turning while the hands are still reaching up to the horizon. The muscles of the back stretch for more, even as the hips stop turning. Then as the knees settle into the barstool position, the left knee changes from pointing inward toward the right knee, and moves toward the target. Some golfers have this as an isolated move of the left knee sent gently out over a flat left foot. Then, the left shoulder moves up, the triangle tilts, and the hands descend so that the right elbow can regain its position at the waist.

While all this subtle stuff is going on below the waist, the question can be asked again when the hands reach the top: What starts the downswing? The simple answer is: The left shoulder. However, the golfer must recognize that the "settling on the barstool" is absolutely essential because it controls your timing for the speed to that point of the golf swing. When the barstool position has been reached, that becomes the signal to accelerate the torso rotation through the ball from this stable platform. For shots that require a reconnection of the right elbow to the waist area—omit this settling process at your peril. Cutting out the settling action—which many think of as a pause—leaves you nothing much more than a "hit from the top" and another disappointing two-handed slash at the ball.

When the knees have settled into the barstool position, the left shoulder will move straight upward, so that three reactions will take place:

1. The right elbow regains its connection to the right hip.
2. Both knees are ready to begin the drive through the impact zone.
3. The left hip gets out of the way by rotating counterclockwise over a flexed left knee.

PHOTO CREDIT: Alvie Thompson

Moe Norman just starting his way back down to the pre-impact position. The left knee is over the flat left foot. The left shoulder begins to move up to tilt the right elbow down to regain connection with the waist. This is an important destination for the golf swing. It can be argued that the success of your shot depends on attaining this posture.

Admittedly, this move made by Hogan and other touring professionals takes some time for study and practice, which you might not be able to find in your schedule. But believe it or not, you can get the hang of it, and practice it daily at work, during a "two minute vacation" in a swivel chair. This drill represents what goes on below the waist from the top of the backswing and down to the pre-impact position.

MIRROR DRILL

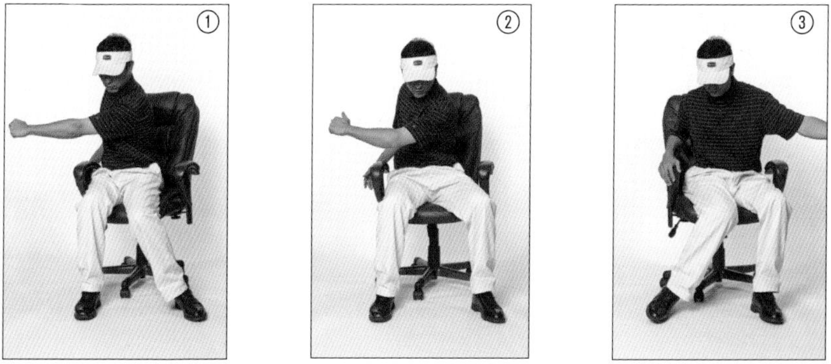

① The left knee moves inward as if to touch the stable right knee while the hands continue to the top of the backswing.

② The left knee then moves out over the left foot's big toe just before the hands stop.

③ The right knee begins its drive under the ball toward the target.

If you take the time to try this leg action, which gets you down from the top and into the barstool position and the pre-impact stage, try it at the office or check in the mirror at home for details.

- Is your left shoulder still past the ball?
- Is your left knee bending in toward the center of the chest? (Not toward the target line.)
- Are you still in the "closed" stance?
- Is your right foot ninety degrees to the target line?

(Stoically, Hogan attended to this right angle foot position for a long time, but found—as you might—that advancing age with its anatomical changes and tightening ligaments and tendons forced him to open that right foot just a bit to accommodate his upper body turn. You could need this tip one day, because if your left shoulder does not point to the ball or behind it, your full shot ball will go to the right of the target. For short shots, you can get around the problem of your left shoulder not being behind the ball—by opening your stance according to the shot required.)

- The last thing to check in the mirror of your first move down from the top is your arm position. The right arm is bent to ninety degrees to accommodate the return of the elbow to the hip area. This will automatically lower the right shoulder a bit. The left arm is straight and held firmly in the supinated position with the dimples pointing skyward.
- You know how the hands look: Both are in dorsi-flexion with the left hand prepared to apply Hogan's secret.

« It is not a good idea to think about the hands when playing. But during your practice you could take time to notice that the right palm points at the ball for the first phase of the takeaway.

Again, don't think about the hands when playing. But at practice you can note that the right palm now faces the target during the follow-through. »

If you have all of these details ready to take to the practice range for a trial—and you are pretty adept at the mirror drill—here's a variation you might enjoy.

PRACTICE TEE ROUTINE: Four shots in a row with increasing distance.

- After a stretching warm-up, begin with a short chip of five yards to a target for the first shot of the day. For this short chip shot, there is no need to use of the knees. The hands don't change. The left shoulder guides the shot. The left shoulder goes up, and impact is made. If you have actually completed your chipping drills for one week, you will be pleasantly surprised by the quality of your first shot of the day because you are likely starting to use ingrained experience while concentrating on the target.
- The next shot will be twenty yards. Increase the shoulder turn to halfway. This extra turn will hinge the wrists at waist level, and will involve the right knee on the way to impact. Accelerate your body turn through the ball.
- The third target will be fifty yards away, so that more turn is required for the pitch. Feel the strong torquing action of the feet, knees, thighs, and the sudden acceleration of the hips at impact. Balance is supported by the flexed knee over the left foot as the right knee tries to touch the left after impact. Sam Snead called this "making a K."
- The fourth target is eighty yards away and will require a three-quarter swing. Turn to a high finish on the "dirty right toe."

As you go through these four shots on the range over and over, you will feel the gradual crescendo of body tempo from the point of balance to the moment of release and through impact (more on impact just up ahead). The follow-through will reach higher and higher as more distance is required. This practice sequence gives you the advantage of preparing for a "new" shot each time you swing on the practice tee instead of just standing there banging away. It also encourages you to have a target in mind for every practice range shot. Hogan had a purpose for every stroke he took. When you fall into this way of practicing golf, you encourage a cerebral approach to the game rather than a mechanical one, and as a result, course management becomes more routine and easier.

Feel free to try this sequence at home in front of a mirror. You will find that the first-phase chip shot is really the miniature of the following longer shots—right up to a full swing.

① Hold the connection of arms to the torso.

② Release the right side.

③ The rotation of the feet knees and hips are emphasized from the barstool position.

④ The hands are in the Hogan mold for a half shot.

⑤ The three quarter shot sees the right elbow disconnect.

⑥ After re-connecting the right elbow, swing through to a full finish on the right toe.

CHAPTER 8

THE MOVE DOWN TO THE PRE-IMPACT POSITION

Hogan's right elbow returned to his right side and acted like a strut to drive the right forearm and hand to the ball and into impact—time after time after time. This foundation creates a platform easy to assume, and steady by nature. Your shot-making reliability derives from a good barstool position.

The golfer who does not settle into the barstool position misses out on timing into the impact zone and invariably "hits from the top." The patience to settle into this key position can be learned. Watch Tiger a few times. You will see the settling, and then the body ripping the club through the ball at a very fast rate.

When the launching platform has been achieved, the right hand and forearm have one simple purpose: to hold the clubhead firmly on its track into the back of the ball with an arched hand as the upper body turns through the ball toward the target.

The right hand is in dorsiflexion for the whole ride and is held in place on the waist area giving the feel for how the right side of the body can push the fulcrum through a full shot.

The right hand is powered through the ball by the effect of the left shoulder rising suddenly, as well as being pushed by the release of the right knee and hip and shoulder with the right heel rising.

The right fulcrum moves the right hand to impact as the torso rotates through the ball.

Stan Leonard demonstrates how the right fulcrum powers the right hand to impact as the torso rotates through the ball.

From shoulder to wrist the left arm is locked in supination. The inner dimples are pointed to the sky to prevent rolling toward the target during impact. The left hand is in dorsi-flexion as it moves toward impact.

THE ROLE OF THE LEFT HAND

The left hand has the main purpose of accelerating the clubface into the ball at the last second of golf's climactic moment—impact. The clubface is held firmly in a position one or two degrees "open"—the result of the dimple of the left arm being turned skyward as the golfer "twists and arches" the left hand. That combination develops the power fade. The connected left arm holds the hand structure from moving during the force of impact because the dimple-skyward position (supination) held strongly resists any further rotation of the arm.

Many tour players warm up with left-handed-chips in order to test their left arm connection with the shoulder, and the strength of their left wrist position. Dick Zokol and John Daly are two practitioners, but perhaps the "king" would be Jerry Pate of Macon, Georgia, who at twenty-two said that he "felt ready to play when he could hit a three wood two hundred yards with his left hand only." He might have been right, because in 1976 at the U.S. Open in Atlanta he needed a bit of strength to clear water from the right rough with a 190 yard five iron. He hit a high ball close. Walking up to his putt he said he felt numb. "'Just hit straight at it as easy as you can.' The ball just barely went in the front. I remember pulling it out and throwing it. I should have kept that ball. It was a Ben Hogan. I wish I had it today."

Just before impact the left hand applies Hogan's Secret. The fingers squeeze, and the hand arches into the ball.

The left shoulder continues to rise as the right side releases and the chest turns over a flexed left knee, and with the left bicep still connected to the torso, the whole unit turns toward the target. The club shaft is in a straight line with the left arm—not the right.

Off the course these one-armed sequences can be repeated a few times daily to revisit those important, isolated movements which occur during the crucial moments of the golf swing. This one-armed form of practice is not onerous, and doesn't take long—of course it might cause the odd raised eyebrow among uninitiated observers—but it can be very effective as a ten second calming break during your day at work. You now need the feeling of the exact timing—so here's just a bit more detail.

THE POINT OF BALANCE

The "point of balance" is a term I was forced to make up—never having heard it mentioned before—but it sure is a great little place. This point along the swing path is attained when, from the barstool position, the golfer raises the left shoulder so that the hands move down to a position above the right knee. The left arm is straight (dimple up) and forms a right angle with the club shaft. There is a lightness and balance to the club at this point, as

Getting in touch with the "point of balance" with lobs from the pre-impact zone. Dimples up—both hands dorsiflexed over right knee.

it is supported by the arm and shoulder triangle which is connected with the torso.

With the tilt still in progress (and we are now slowing this detailed description down to super-slow-motion, which is why we have to read it, feel it, then ingrain it, before putting it into use on the course), the left shoulder continues to rise. Knees, hips, and chest keep rotating toward the target, and the hands, still in dorsiflexion, are being moved by the triangle while the left hand arches into the solid arched structure designed for impact. Within those few inches down the infield to a position above the left knee, the secret is applied and the whole right side powers through the ball. This is a very athletic move as the stored up power is released into the ball, and the golfer turns square to the target, up on the right toe with hands reaching down the target line.

Moving to impact with the twist and arch action.

THE MOMENT OF TRUTH

At impact, the left arm is strongly connected to the rib cage—and with long-shafted clubs, the left arm could appear to be stretched across the chest. It is still holding the ninety degree angle of the arms with the club shaft. In spite of all the speed developing . . . and despite running out of room (as one touring pro said, "It feels like I've gone past the ball") a new special little action occurs as the hands reach the left knee: "*El momento de la verdad.*"

A surge through the ball as fast and as strong as the torso can turn. This golfer will be up on his right toe in a moment.

So here we are at last: The Moment of Truth for every golfer. The left hand changes from dorsiflexion to arched palmar flexion. And there it is: Hogan's "secret move" with the left hand, that nobody could see. The secret occurs just as the strongly constructed triangle of arms and shoulders tilt the clubhead through the ball while the torso turns with great force and accelerating speed.

However, what has really happened? Just before arching the left hand into impact, the swing has reached the point where something has to give—as when you came to the difference between the follow-through for a short putt, and the follow-through for a long putt. The lower body has to release in order to keep the upper body's triangle intact, with the butt end of the club's grip still between the shoulders. The shoulder line can then remain parallel to the target line, with the center of your chest behind the ball for a significant time, so that the right shoulder goes under the ball, and not spinning out-of-control "over the top."

Try this movement in slow motion: With your hands over the right knee, raise the left shoulder with both knees holding their flex, and you will see the hands move across the infield to a position above the left knee. At the same time, move the right side (knee and hip) under the ball—just as you apply Hogan's secret. There will be that athletic surge, and you will feel what striking the ball is all about.

It could be said that this explosive release results from the crescendo of minute events leading to the climax of all previous posturing no matter how different from "classical" swings—just like those of Moe Norman, Chi Chi Rodriguez, Miller Barber, and Jim Furyk, to name a few.

Impacting the ball is the main focus of tournament golfers, and a look at the white knuckles on Hogan's left hand may cause you to question the value of that old instruction: "Hold the club as if you had two canaries in your hands." It is hoped that this book will stimulate you to try the strong molded hands of golfing giants such as Ben Hogan, Sam Snead, Stan Leonard, or Tiger Woods, and watch closely the way good golfers hold the club through the impact zone.

Feeling this point of balance and release is probably best experienced using the tempo employed by Ernie Els during his half-wedge shots.

Of course for the lob shot, a V swing is used for the takeaway, which moves the clubhead upward abruptly . . . instead of the U swing which has the normal extension back down the target line away from the ball.

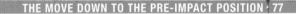

PHOTO CREDIT: Getty Images

Hogan at the Moment of Truth with his hands about to apply the twist and arch of his secret. If you've ever heard that you should grip the club as if holding a bird, check out the white knuckles on Hogan's left hand.

Hogan's left hip is moving out of the way. The right elbow has re-attached as a fulcrum to the right side. His left shoulder is about to thrust straight upwards and the right knee is ready to drive with speed under the point established by the left shoulder. His posture is steady as a rock.

You will feel how easy it is to turn the right knee and hip through the ball with the arch and twist when everything is timed by the upward thrust of the left shoulder and the turning torso. There is a definite point of release; when you get the feel for it, you have the timing of the most crucial and fastest part of the golf swing down to the split second.

HOMEWORK

For the fifteen minutes before dinner is served, here's my favorite "stolen" practice time in the backyard—or any spot that's handy. Try to keep the club shaft as an extension of the left arm through the ball and not as an extension of the right—which would indicate a breaking down of the arched left wrist. Holding the shaft as an extension of the left arm is possible because tension in the hips is released by the turning right knee—this allows the left writst to remain strongly arched and not collapsing.

PHOTO CREDIT: Helen Hunt

PHOTO CREDIT: Helen Hunt

CHAPTER 9

HOGAN AT IMPACT

Once down to the barstool position, with a stable flat-footed stance and knees flexed for strength, Hogan was ready for the object of the whole golf exercise—impact. Everything else has been a prelude to this moment, however brief it may be. Some get to this key position quicker than others, but speed is not important before this important posture.

The first takeaway from the address position can be fluid and methodical. The raising of the hands to the top of the backswing can be pedestrian, languid—Els-like. Too many golfers begin the downswing, from the top, with a wild slash of the club with as much velocity as they can muster—speed is really unnecessary until you are in Hogan's barstool position (as just discussed above) and ready for impact. Some golfers swing solely from this knee-settling position. Remember Doug Sanders? Just about won the British Open at St. Andrews. They used to say that he could swing in a telephone booth. My point is that some play golf with the satisfaction of hitting the ball solidly despite going no further than half way back, because the barstool is the engine room of the golf swing. Here is where the speed of the club is unleashed by an accelerating turn of the torso, with the right side driving through the ball—once the point of balance has been achieved. (Perhaps "point of attack" would be appropriate too.)

BACK IN TIME

Jay Hebert visited Vancouver for the BC Centennial Open at Point Grey in 1958 and I was fortunate enough to shag balls for the man who had been wounded in the battle for Iwo Jima when a captain in the Marine Corps. I knew that Hebert had taken up photography during his rehabilitation, and was a friend of Hogan's.

When Hogan came to a golf clinic at Moon Brook Country Club in Jamestown, New York, in 1953 Jay asked Hogan if he "could take a couple of pictures." Without the luxury of modern high-speed cameras, Jay snapped away—trying to decipher the mystery of Hogan's hands at impact. Interestingly enough, Curt Sampson wrote in *Hogan* that following the clinic, Hogan asked Jay for a ride to the train depot where, without announcing his intentions, Hogan began his journey to Scotland to play in the British Open at Carnoustie. It is pleasing to note that these pictures were taken just days after Hogan's impressive U.S. Open victory at Oakmont, and only weeks before his decisive win at Carnoustie. Furthermore, we must recognize that these images caught the master at work at the peak of his career. (We are grateful that Jay's son Jean-Paul and his brother Jason believed the photographs would serve golf history more favorably in a book rather than a bureau drawer.)

PHOTO CREDIT: Jay Hebert

The right elbow rejoins the right hip.

And, after all those years, here are those images from the past for us to view. As blurry as the details of these fifty-seven year old pictures are, we can make out a sequence through the all-im-

PHOTO CREDIT: Jay Hebert

Flexed knees begin a strong rotation while the left shoulders drives upwards and the hands arrive over the right knee and the point of balance.

PHOTO CREDIT: Jay Hebert

The hands move across the infield to the point of release over the left knee.

portant impact zone which Hebert was trying to record for analysis. Note Hogan's strong turn of the Magical Device rotating toward the target. We can follow the control of the left shoulder as it tilts the triangle.

The point of release occurs during a special moment on the pre-impact swing wherein the weight of the club is negligible. This moment allows the convex or dorsiflexed left hand to arch and twist into Hogan's secret with an effortless move while still ahead of the clubhead at impact. It is also in concert with the rotating torso above a stable and flexed left knee, and an athletic drive by the right side: knee, hip, and shoulder.

PHOTO CREDIT: Jay Hebert

Impact with hands in the twist and arch position.

Tiger shows the loose hands of a waggle while just loosening up, getting a feel for the tempo required for this particular shot while imagining the ball's flight as Hogan did.

PHOTO CREDIT: Mike Lilly

HOGAN'S PRE-SWING WAGGLE

Hogan knew people were trying their best to discover his secret and he played to their interest by saying, "The secret is right in front of you, but you have to know where to look." There is no doubt among those who knew him well that he delighted in this teasing game because he believed it would lead to "big money" some day. Stan Leonard pointed out that Hogan had often told him, "Never give it away, Stan. Make them pay for it. It comes from your hard work."

Now that you know what the secret is, you can also see it in his waggle. Leonard said (in different words) that Hogan got the feel of going from dorsiflexion to palmar flexion two or three times before addressing the ball, just to spark muscle memory for the timing of the left hand at the point of release.

Everyone automatically assumed—by the "handsy" way that Hogan waggled the club away from the ball—that he also used the same action for the takeaway. The waggle was a pronation with the left hand, which opened the clubface on the way back. And because no one knew that his left hand used the twist and arch of palmar flexion, they thought that he had swung back over the ball by pronating his right hand. But this was not the case. And that's where trouble began for the thousands who made that assumption.

In his book, *Five Lessons*, Hogan stated: "During the waggle the shoulders do not turn. On the actual swing they do. The hands, arms, and the shoulders start to move almost simultaneously on the backswing."

Hogan's takeaway was accomplished by means of tilting the arm and shoulder triangle—just as you have practiced with putting, through chipping, and to the full shots—not by moving his hands. For the takeaway, the hands are part of the triangle and stay in place. In sharp contrast, the golfer's hands move by themselves during the practice swing waggle. For your own good, please understand the differences between Hogan's proper take-away, which was a shoulder tilt for the first two feet, and a waggle for a feel of where the wrists arch.

PHOTO CREDIT: Mike Lilly

Tiger shows the triangle action for the takeaway. It is now coming to light that Tiger has been studying Hogan's swing. He stated: "I want to own my own swing. Only two players have ever owned their golf swings. One was Ben Hogan and the other was Moe Norman."

CHAPTER 10

TURNING THROUGH THE BALL

It is important to keep the left knee flexed and moving toward the target until impact is over. At that point the upper body turns toward the target over a flexed left knee. As the upper body continues to turn, the right knee—driving under the ball—begins to straighten. The left knee remains flexed until the hands get to waist-high—then, it too begins to straighten.

Tiger used to time his moment of impact with a sudden straightening of the left knee. This action was supposed to get him another four or five yards. Unfortunately, all it got him were three arthroscopic knee operations which may or may not come back to haunt him with arthritis in the future.

This trick to increase yardage does not help direction at all, and it certainly works against the reliability of the strike. It was first used successfully by the British women's top professional Laura Davies. She was the first European to top the LPGA money list, and she won the U.S. Women's Open in 1987 and holds a career total of sixty-seven victories. The effect on Laura's knees by straightening them at impact is not known. And not trying to be cheeky, but this Coventry lass obviously had been playing soccer during childhood days with her brothers—she

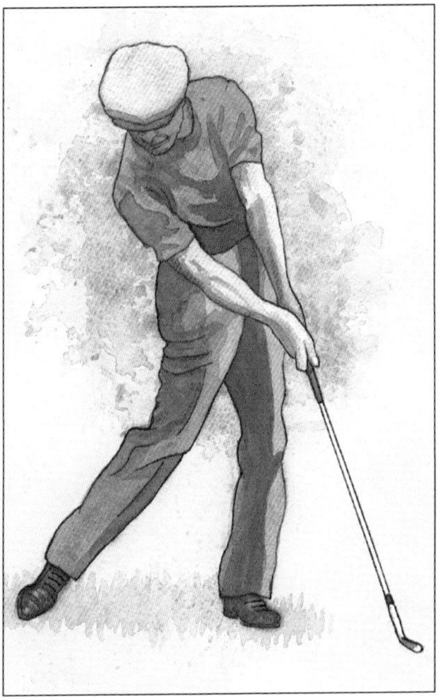

Hogan's hands remain between the turning shoulders and are still in the arched position. Note that the left knee remains flexed even after impact.

certainly has very sturdy pins reminiscent of the legs of a snooker table.

Now we all want to hit the ball longer, but amateurs who try to jump-start the ball by straightening their knees flirt with disaster. That ball could go anywhere because the club arc is all over the place. Play it smart and keep your left knee flexed right through the swing until the time to stand up for the full finish. With stability achieved, you impact the ball from a steady platform, and you have a good chance of placing the clubface squarely on the back of the ball.

As the time of impact approaches, the hips have turned out of the way to clear a path for the hands. The belt buckle is turning rapidly toward the target indicating that the lower body is heading for full release.

The full release of the upper torso is imminent, because we can see that

Tiger on the seventh hole at Thousand Oaks, his right hand still in dorsiflexion. The toe of the club is square to the target line. His nose remains behind the ball's tee position. From this point he will begin standing up for the full follow-through.

PHOTO CREDIT: Mike Lilly

Hogan's knees are still flexed and his left shoulder is at its highest point and straight up from the ground. The club is an extension of his left arm down the target line. Now he can stand up into the full follow-through where his shoulders will be parallel to the ground and his knees straightened.

PHOTO CREDIT: Getty Images

Tiger's head is just beginning to follow the ball's flight which is a forerunner to the chest squaring to the target, just like the hips.

The left shoulder has pulled the triangle to this point, and is now starting to lower to the left, while the right shoulder will rise to bring both shoulders to a horizontal position.

Annika Sorenstam, the great Swedish champion who has ninety professional wins to her record, visited Point Grey in 2003 for the Canadian Women's Open. She allowed her head to rotate through the ball at impact, in concert with her sternum. Like David Duval and Lee Westwood, she believed that by not restricting the head from turning well past impact as Hogan did, her lower body would be able to clear with greater speed for distance. The effect would be that her right ear would be facing the ball at impact rather than the nose—which was Hogan's posture.

When he heard Annika's rationale, Stan Leonard argued that with Hogan's nose-behind-the-ball position, there was a stronger hit past the chin and under the head. His preferred posture enabled golfers like Hogan and Leonard (at five foot eight inches in height) to be the long ball hitters that they were.

Another indication of how Hogan kept his head down was Leonard's assertion that Hogan's whiskers would "rough-up" the collar of his golf shirt while playing.

During his swing-through, Hogan also made certain that his left hand was in full control of the clubface because of its arched position. The right hand followed along for the ride—rather than dominating—and held its arch in extension for as

Slightly further through the swing Moe Norman's hands still hold their arch while pointing to the target. The right arm straightens, and the shoulders are now parallel to the ground. The right elbow is pulled off the waist area, but the arms still maintain strong connection with the torso and that clubhead sure hasn't rolled over.

PHOTO CREDIT: RCGA

long as possible down the line toward the target. This extension of the straightening right arm allowed the clubface to remain looking at the target for a moment longer to give every chance of the ball reflecting the correct angle of the clubface—which was looking directly at the target.

Television commentator Peter Allis wrote of Hogan in *Who's Who in Golf*:

"No one before or since has matched the low drive through the hitting area with his right hand that was the hallmark of the Hogan swing. He had reached perhaps the nearest any golfer has come to mastery over the ball."

CHAPTER 11

FULL FOLLOW-THROUGH TO THE SETTLED POSITION

When the hands reach waist-high on the swing-through, the stand-up process can begin. The hips turn to square with the target, and the right side has "released" completely under the ball. The full release of the right side is demonstrated by a turn of the hips which results in the belt buckle facing the target and a "dirty right toe" upon which the golfer is nicely balanced. From this comfortable position the golfer can turn his head and watch the ball's journey towards the target with calm affection—just like the big boys do.

A high finish is the deceleration and natural ending to a full swing. The balance began at the first address position and is still apparent in the finishing position.

When his swing to the top for a high finish was complete, Hogan would settle back, allowing his arms to drop while he studied the flight of the ball. His elbows would bend but he would not relax his hands, which were molded into their impact position. Of course this attention to detail was not surprising to close friends, to whom it was known that Hogan used his golf grip even on his knife and fork while eating. Ernie Brown was a friendly head professional at Vancouver's Quilchena Golf Club. He was also a crack player who grew up in the Great Depression as Stan Leonard's friend. Both caddies, they would sneak on to Shaughnessy Heights Golf Club whenever there was enough moonlight to find the ball.

On holiday, following World War II, Ernie drove down to Los Angeles to try his luck on the "Gold Trail" and there met Ben Hogan, who had traveled from Texas by train. After the tournament, Ernie offered Hogan a ride to Portland, the next tour stop, and after winning in Oregon, the usually taciturn Hogan became more friendly as they drove up the Pacific Coast to Seattle. By the time they reached their third stop in Vancouver, Hogan suggested to Ernie: "How 'bout fixing that grip of yours a bit? Get that left thumb down the shaft a little. Arch both hands when you lob, and move them with your arms hugging your body right through the finish."

Hogan described to Brown the need for strong connection of both elbows hugging the rib cage for lobs around the green. The importance of staying connected by hugging the rib cage with the biceps is recognized by Vijay Singh, with his

CPGA professional Ernie Brown showing what Hogan taught him on the way home from Hogan's win at the Portland Open in 1945.

PHOTO CREDIT: Shirley Brown

glove tucked under his left armpit for practice in "staying connected." He might have learned this trick from Babe Ruth, who put his cap under his left arm for batting practice. Also strong on this connection point is Padraig Harrington, winner of the British Open in 2007 with a follow-up victory in 2008 and a win at the PGA Championship to finish off a banner year. Harrington has gloves under both arms for practice, making certain he is turning a connected torso through his short irons.

The special focus for Hogan at impact is how close the elbows are to each other, and the fact that the dimples on the inside of both elbows are pointing to the sky. The right elbow is connected just above right hip joint, and is a valuable contact point acting as a fulcrum as the hips turn and help guide, and even push, the hands toward impact. Let us be certain here, that any push by the hands is done in a special way—strongly connected to the torso, with any push being done only with the heel of the right hand against the heel of the left hand. In this way the strong fingers of the right hand never collapse the left wrist.

MEMORIES TO SWING BY

The swing to a high finish during a practice swing is a good muscle memory for the golfer to feel just before his swing at the ball. For example, by holding hands high at address—as Moe Norman does for an instant before beginning his swing—the golfer has a lingering feel for where he wants to be after the shot—and swings back to that position guided by that memory.

Moe Norman did away with Hogan's first stage of the takeaway by simply assuming the recommended position at address—with the clubhead a foot or more behind the ball and with no risk of a change in the hand position for impact. Moe explained that he did not want to risk taking the clubhead too far "inside" where the club could get "stuck behind" in a position where the shaft was not parallel to the target line. As Tiger Woods warned: "From behind, it is almost impossible to return the clubface squarely to the ball." So it was from this new starting point back down the target line that Moe hinged his wrists parallel to the target line, from approximately the same place as did Hogan and Nicklaus.

Stan Leonard would take two enjoined practice swings—half back, away from the ball—then a slow swing to halfway through, while rehearsing his torso turn

Moe Norman's swing was idiosyncratic but Hogan praised the unyielding hand position for impact.

PHOTO CREDIT: RCGA

and the timing of his left hand arch. This preliminary action was followed by a swing back down the target line—away from the ball to waist-high—then a body turn through the ball up to the top where the proper balanced position was felt, held for a second . . . and remembered. Quickly back to address position, he'd imagine the ball's flight . . . then the hit, and back up to the rehearsed follow-through position.

PHOTO CREDIT: Mike Lilly

Tiger's athletic follow-through under the scrutiny of his caddy, Steve Williams—no doubt the wealthiest bagger in the world.

Hogan at practice in arguably the most important position for solid, consistent contact. Note that the right elbow has returned to the hip. The left hand is in dorsi-flexion. Hips and knees are turning the torso to contact over a stable, flexed knee.

CHAPTER 12

TEN STAGES OF HOGAN'S SWING IN SERIATIM

For a review of the stages of Ben Hogan's swing, let's take a look at ten key positions within Hogan's action. The golfer is Rose-Mary Basham of Point Grey, whose swing looks a lot like a young Hogan without the cap. Rose-Mary is a Vancouver lawyer who represents a new breed of club member: ladies with a full membership as part owners. Women were once relegated to play any other day but Saturday and only certain times on Sundays, in order to accommodate male members who theoretically could not play during the week because of work. But Rose-Mary worked all week herself and wanted to golf on the weekends—so she politely asked, "Why?" She was told, just as politely, that it was because she was not a "full member" as ladies paid only half the usual entrance fee which obviated them from owning a "share" in the club as a company.

"That's the reason I'm treated like a second-class member without full privileges?" she asked.

"That's it," came the answer.

"How much to change that?" was her response.

The amount was named. The check was cleared. That next Saturday, working woman Rose-Mary went to the pro shop looking for a game, and was sent by the starter to the first tee. Here, three grinning men welcomed her to what was heretofore a working man's tee-off time.

The first club tournament for full-play members was the Fall Chariot. This year-ending soiree was usually for men only, but Rose-Mary played, just for the cheek of it. She—and others watching—wanted the satisfaction of doing it once, in order to break a seventy-five year history of exclusion. She was told by one grump

① A good, solid looking foundation ready for an athletic swing. Right elbow on the waist. Right knee steady and flexed. Hands anticipating impact.

② Only the triangle moves, pushed by the left shoulder. That the hands do not move by themselves is demonstrated by the fact the back of the left hand (and the right palm) are angled down to the ground behind the ball. Imagine a clubhead in the palm of your right hand and see how it fits the angle of the clubhead on the ground. This gives the right brain a powerful image to contemplate.

③ The right knee is flexed and steady with most of the weight on the inside edge of the shoe. As the left knee is pulled in toward the center of the body line, the upper body turns away from the target. The continued push of the left shoulder raises the arms until they are parallel to the target line. The back of the left hand has not moved or rotated—it faces the target line. Only now do the wrists begin to hinge into dorsiflexion.

④ The left shoulder keeps pushing the arms and hands higher. Wrists hinge fully, and both hands are in dorsiflexion at the top.

that he didn't "think this was right." Rose-Mary just smiled and asked sweetly, "I made the cut—did you?" He hadn't of course, and just to make it sweeter, Rose-Mary, with a handful of tickets, won six out of the seven draw prizes! She also won the long drive competition for her handicap group. That went over like a lead balloon, so . . . lo and behold, next spring, the opening day tournament had been renamed the Men's Chariot Race. This change thus made Rose-Mary the first, and last lady, to crack the gender-based tournament schedule.

⑤ Although the hips stop their clockwise rotation at a quarter of a turn (forty-five degrees), the torso progresses to a half a turn, as the hands are pushed toward the top. Before the club shaft reaches the horizon, the left knee is moved back over the left foot and as the hands stretch to the top.

⑥ The first objective for the initial move down is to regain connection with the right elbow onto the hip area. So in order to come down, the left shoulder turns at an angle toward the target line with the golfer's back to the target, as the lower body settles into the barstool position.

⑦ Here the golfer is in a solid foundation for the climax to all the work. This is the engine room of golf, where the torso (or core muscles of the thighs, abdomen, hips, and buttocks) power the clubface into the ball. The hands are both in dorsi-flexion. The rise of the left shoulder signals the hips to rotate with speed, with the right knee, hip, and shoulder driving under the ball and under the highest point the left shoulder reaches. (The right shoulder does not move toward the target line, but stays on the infield side of the ball.) The hands approach the point of balance.

⑧ As the left hand reaches the point of release near the left knee, Hogan's secret is applied. The long left thumb snaps into an arch with a palmar twist of the last three fingers of the left hand. The dorsiflexed right hand arches, and this new molded hand structure is driven through the ball by the clockwise rotation of the torso. The right elbow as a fulcrum guides the palm of the right hand through the ball as the right side drives down the infield.

⑨ The flexed right knee drives under the ball, while the chest rotates around the spine over a flexed left knee. (Straightening either knee anywhere on the down swing and through impact pulls the golfer's right shoulder "over the top" and a poor shot will result.) The triangle, attached to the turning chest, keeps the hands between the shoulders to extend down the target line. The left hand is in a strong palmarflexion position. The right hand is now in a lessened but still strong dorsiflexion position, because of the stretch down the target line which—if a full shot—might pull the right elbow across the abdomen and slightly off the right hip area.

⑩ The through-swing toward the target after impact is a mirror of the backswing away from the ball. In both instances the golfer rotates through the impact zone with the chest and shoulders parallel to the target line. After contact, the chest turns toward the target and squares the line across the shoulders and hips to face the target. The right side releases fully, so that the right foot has turned with the heel fully off the ground to a position called the "dirty right toe." Now the left leg can straighten. The belt buckle (or the navel—take your pick) is turned to face the target. The old pros said to "hold this pose for the photographer for two seconds."

CHAPTER 13

REVIEWING THE SECRET

At this juncture we should take another look at the long sought after, and the oft' misunderstood—Hogan's Secret. His Magical Device gives the golfer accuracy by means of "connected strength." Hogan's Secret accelerates the power stored for impact like no other attempt at acceleration can. An arm-swing speed-up can't come close. A faster leg drive can get things out of control. Hogan's secret is highly effective, and is the tool that touring pros have been vague to secretive about for fifty-five years that I know about—except a few are now saying after the publication of *Ben Hogan's Magical Device*—"That's what I meant."

The only movement in Hogan's hands was the change of the left from a convex arch at address to concave dorsiflexion when raised above the waist by a shoulder tilt on the backswing. And then, just before impact, the left hand returned to the arched position of palmar flexion, for strength through the ball at impact. Several touring professionals such as Palmer and Trevino adopted this impact position—not that they credited, or copied, Hogan's Secret. They didn't, because there was no way they could perceive this move, given that cameras of those days could not freeze the impact without a blur—so they could never be certain. They merely found themselves a hand position that resisted breaking down, and they searched

PHOTO CREDIT: B.C. Golf House

Wayne Vollmer showing strong hand position on his final shot of the 1971 BC Open with an 85 yard pitching wedge on the 421 yard, par four eighteenth hole at Marine Drive Golf Club with an eagle two for the win.

it out by trial and error. Arnold Palmer said that "he and his dad figured it out."

The difference I found with some of the pros was that they would squeeze the last three fingers of the left hand, but they might not put an arched wrist with it. Under pressure, low hands meant a flatter swing plane, and back would come that nasty unwanted hook, in what they called a "double cross."

Wayne Vollmer, the head professional at Morgan Creek Golf Course in Surrey, British Columbia, won the BC Open in 1971. By happenstance, I met Vollmer on the practice fairway at Point Grey on the Saturday afternoon before his final Sunday round. We said hello, and he acknowledged my guests by giving them an imitation of Lee Trevino's swing, then one of Palmer's. When my playing partners started asking him for swing tips, I pulled them away, not wanting Wayne to lose any focus. Glad we left, I thought the next day when Wayne sunk an eighty-five yard pitching wedge on the final hole at Marine Drive Golf Club to win the BC Open.

A few days later, Wayne, still pumped, admitted that he needed to hit a long drive on the final hole because his opponent was safely down the middle, and Wayne figured a birdie would be required just to remain tied.

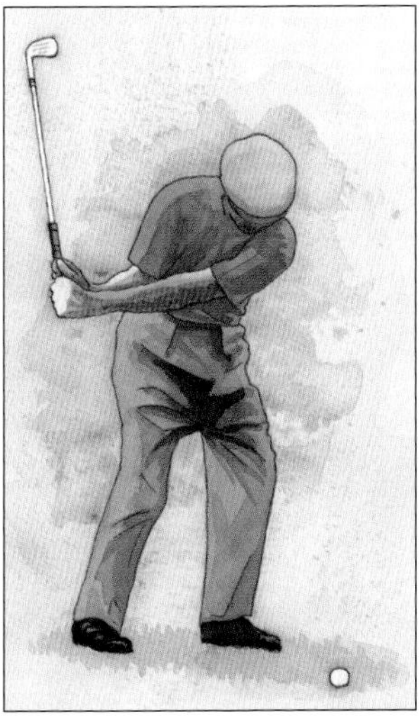

Hogan in the pre-impact position where the club never deviates from its intended path because of the strong platform he develops with the connected triangle for this torso-powered shot.

The trouble was his fear of pull-hooking the ball because there was out of bounds down the left side, the full length of the hole. "I squeezed those last three fingers of my left hand so hard they just about cramped . . . . I learned that from Hogan."

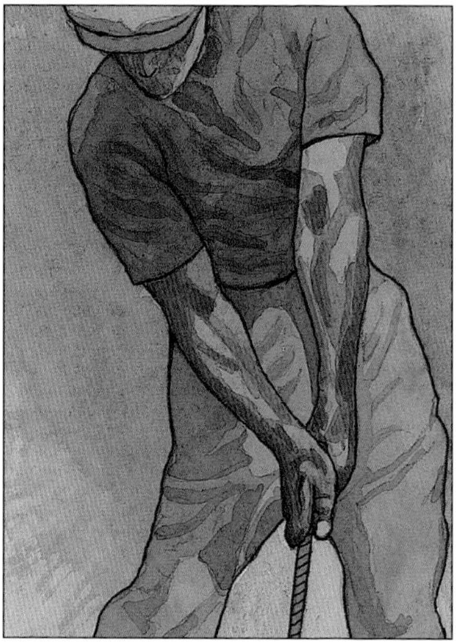

You can call the wrist buckled, call it bulging, or convex—but don't call it supination, because that is exactly what Hogan did not want to do with the left hand. So, let's be clear: It is the left arm that is in supination, and this position is held firmly throughout the swing when Hogan wanted a fading ball. He did not want a rolling left hand, or arm, which could "double-cross" his intention. The right hand is held in concave dorsiflexion throughout the swing. It is only the left hand that moves from dorsiflexion to palmar flexion at impact—with a twist and arch.

Keen-eyed Johnny Miller, the noted television announcer, came the closest of all the pros to determining what Hogan's secret when he stated that he thought it was: "the way he buckled his wrist into the ball." I'm sure Miller could have demonstrated what he meant by "buckled" because he had an impressive golf career of his own, including a win at 1973 U.S. Open championship at Oakmont in Pennsylvania—even after he forgot his yardage book for the Saturday round, a mistake resulting in a disastrous seventy-six. The next day, however, he won handily by shooting a course record sixty-three. He also won the British Open at Royal Birkdale in 1976. So, if Johnny Miller said "buckled," I was ready to listen.

In February 1972, at the Bing Crosby National Pro-Am at Pebble Beach, I was determined to ask Miller about his Hogan thoughts, but could not seem to catch him with a quiet moment. Tour players have a crowded and routine-filled daily schedule and are constantly approached by fans with interrupting questions. To make matters worse—perhaps impossible—Miller tied for first place in the Sunday round with the pre-eminent Jack Nicklaus, but still, I thought that "maybe after. . . ." No such luck though.

The first play-off hole was back on the par four fifteenth coming out of a tree-lined chute. Both hit good drives but Miller, with very active legs, hit his second shot on the hosel of a seven iron, and we watched the ball heading down Seventeen Mile Drive getting further out of bounds with each bounce. So I never got to ask exactly what he meant by "buckle."

Hogan himself showed Anthony Ravielli, the artist, how the left hand was held for impact. It was just that Hogan described the development of this position with terms of "pronation" and "supination" for the hands. And these actions did not apply to Hogan when using his secret for the power fade. His left hand impact position is more correctly described as palmar flexion, with an arched wrist as Hogan pressed his long left thumb down the shaft to the ball. This strong structure is more likely to respond with the expected result—a power fade which "falls to the right."

To apply Hogan's secret, here is a sequence from the top of the backswing to the position ready to unleash the stored up power. You should be able to run through this sequence like a World Cup slalom racer tracing the course in his mind's eye. You can do this anywhere—in the dentist's chair, or waiting on a tee. The best time is when your head is on the pillow just as you are about to fade off. Let's imagine using the secret for a fifty yard lob shot.

① The blade is slightly open at address.

② The left shoulder pushes down and raises the hands on a V swing, sharply to the top. The right elbow remains attached to the golfer's side. The left bicep is pressed to the chest. The left arm is held in supination from address to finish. The wrists are fully hinged and both hands are dorsiflexed.

③ Coming back to the ball, both knees shift toward the target when the left shoulder lifts straight up towards the golfer's ear. This move with the knees toward the target is done with an unhurried tempo. The clubhead, in a controlled crescendo, accelerates on the way to the ball with the turning of the torso . . . the left shoulder raises straight up—still parallel to the target line—and this rise of the shoulder tilts the triangle, which in turn brings the arching left hand, and the still dorsiflexed (concave) right hand, firmly accelerating into the ball. At impact, the dimples of both elbows point to the sky so that there is no rolling by either arm. They are part of the connected triangle, and move in concert with the turning torso.

④ The triangle is firmly connected to the torso, and therefore, the hands remain between the shoulders as the chest turns through the ball. Flexed knees continue rotating the belt buckle toward the target. The torso does not slide toward the target—the hips rotate counter-clockwise and away from the target line.

⑤ Hands are still in front and pointing at the target, as is the center of the chest in a follow-through—abbreviated here, only because it is not a full shot.

CHAPTER 14

SPECIALTY SHOTS

The power fade was the end result of Hogan's development of the Magical Device along with the application of his secret.

The Magical Device, or the way the triangle is connected to the rotating torso, keeps the hands from taking over the golf swing—because when they do, they most usually change the angle of the clubface into the ball . . . and of course the object is to keep that clubface held constant for as long as possible through impact, so that the compressed ball can actually cling to the stable face for an instant, and then leave it, reflecting the intended path to the target with the intended spin. Hogan applied controlled ball trajectory to his repertoire as well.

The stimulus for Hogan to undertake this whole complex and detailed analysis for an overhaul of his swing, was undertaken because when he was a caddy with Byron Nelson—his only friend as a twelve-year-old—there was a caddy shack game they played called "Hit for a Chase." The caddy who hit his drive the shortest was forced to pick up all the other balls. Now Ben was 130 pounds and five foot nine as an adult. You can imagine him as a runt kid who was picked on relentlessly by all the other caddies except Byron who stuck up for Bennie.

Byron almost always won the game; Bennie almost always lost. He even tried to hit the ball cross-handed, until the pro taught him a strong grip (like Azinger's) so he could hit a hard-running hook on that dried-out Texas turf. This was the hook that would haunt his first years as a professional.

It took Hogan ten years to finally win a tournament in 1940 after turning pro at seventeen. Tiger required but three months during his first year for his first win. Hogan won six events in a row in 1948 at age thirty-six. Tiger tied Hogan with six in a row in 2000 at age twenty-five. Such was the difference in their early years of development.

Hogan's reaction to his lack of early progress was to construct a new swing which would allow him to never again fear an over-the-top duck hook with its severe penalties both mental and physical.

The product of all his work was the ability to hit a power fade which eliminated trouble on the left side of the fairway, and made him a fearless shot-maker who put the ball where he wanted it. When playing the majestic eighteenth hole at Pebble Beach, where the world's largest lateral water hazard looms on the left and brings competitors to inward retching, Hogan simply hit the ball as hard as he could down the line of surf crashing against the sea wall, so that he could reach the par five finishing hole in two.

PHOTO CREDIT: Ken West

The barstool position from where the effects of a strong or weak grip are applied along with the action of the hands to spin the ball left or right.

HITTING THE POWER FADE

You've been practicing all the parts:

- The left arm is held with the dimple pointing skyward. This prevents the arm from rolling over—during and through impact.
- The right hand is held in dorsiflexion so that it will not release from this arched position and collapse the weaker long-left-thumb grip of the left hand.
- The left hand is arched with a twist into a very strong structure, like a fist that will not break down.

A slightly closed blade whose sweet spot approaches the ball's imagined center from slightly inside the target line puts a "right to left" (counter-clockwise) spin to the ball. A slightly open blade whose sweet spot approaches the ball's center from slightly outside the target line puts a "left to right" spin to the ball.

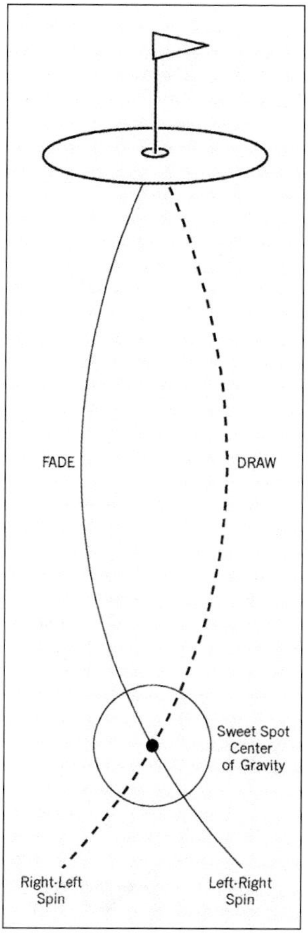

The combination of these three detailed parts of the Magical Device holds the clubhead on its path toward the ball without any change to the angle of the clubface. And because of the long-left-thumb grip on the handle, the clubface—as controlled by the leading edge of the blade—is held, automatically, one or two degrees open. Certainly, there is never a hint of the face closing.

Thus a great advantage is created by using Hogan's system. For approach shots to the green, an accurate shot to the intended target is expected. But what about stopping the damned thing when it gets there? In the next chapter we talk about the slightly open face through contact with the ball that produces a "left to right" (clockwise) spin to the ball, which will tend to bring the ball to a quicker stop.

PLAYING THE DRAW SHOT

At times the player will want the opposite "right to left" spin on the ball in order to create a draw. This close relative of the hook has its dangers—what in golf doesn't?—and there are times when you will want the ball to hit and roll a considerable distance on a green, whether for a long chip, or a punched three-quarter shot.

Let's take a full pitching wedge as an example—pros call this a "scoring club." With the pin a long way back in the left hand corner of the green, you want to land on the right hand side of the green as Hogan instructed, and let it draw into the center-left portion at the back.

1. Take a stronger left hand grip by moving the knuckle of the left forefinger—the only one you can see at address—and turn it clockwise on the shaft so that you can now see two knuckles.
2. Set the dimple of the left arm to point inward toward the torso's center, then turn this new set-up by means of the triangle.
3. Swing as usual.

When he wanted a "draw shot" Hogan called his procedure "changing the chuck on the lever."

Nicklaus said that he himself didn't change his hands; he merely changed the face of the club. When his target called for a draw

« Moe Norman slings the clubface into the ball with his extended right hand creating right to left spin for a draw shot. The tell tale sign for a draw is that—through the ball—the club shaft is an extension of the right arm. A fade is produced when the club is an extension of the left. Here Norman's left wrist is in only moderate dorsi-flexion because the left elbow dimple is held strongly towards the center of the chest and prevents the left hand from excessive dorsi-flexion as in a collapse.

PHOTO CREDIT: RCGA

Camilo Villegas, who honed his golf at the University of Florida before winning three PGA Tour events, is very much Hogan's size and rips the ball as Hogan did. Here with a strong grip and the left elbow dimple pointing inwards across the chest to promote a moderate left arm supination, he sets up for a draw at the Thousand Oaks Invitational. »

PHOTO CREDIT: Mike Lilly

Nicklaus set up his body lines to the right, then "closed" the clubface a touch by aiming the sweet spot of the club at the pin, and then swung normally.

At quarter to six one chilly morning at the Pebble Beach polo grounds serving as the practice range for the Crosby, Nicklaus opined that he really only "thought about" drawing the ball. In a private moment while the caddies were away finding coffee, Nicklaus chuckled that when he was playing well, he could imagine a pencil line drawn from the ball up and through the air to the landing spot he intended. He said it felt like cheating in art class by tracing—he just swung down that pencil line that was so vivid for him. Strangely enough, a few years earlier, Fred Couples had given the same explanation for playing a draw: "I just think about it."

Stan Leonard, PGA Player of the Year in 1959, was horrified that anyone (even Nicklaus the man with more victories in "major championships at eighteen; four more wins than Tiger and eight or nine more than Hogan") would change the position of the club. Leonard preferred Hogan's method with, at times, one more addition. "If you really have to bend one," Stan said confidentially, "Let the left shoulder move with the left hip and pull 'away' from the target line—instead of moving straight up to the sky. You pull away just as you're going to contact the ball—but don't straighten the knee or else."

This kernel of "inside" advice came after I had flushed a shot during a twilight practice round where we hit two balls: Leonard playing an imagined game against Ben Hogan, and me playing against Hogan's arch-rival Sam Snead. After I had smacked this ball straight down the center of the sixteenth at Point Grey, Leonard growled, "Goddamned hacker."

Taken by surprise, I pursued his comment by explaining: "Pro, I really tagged that one." I was even more surprised by the passionate retort. "This dogleg hole calls for a draw for position to the green. You aim down the right side and bring it into the center ten thousand times out of ten thousand times just short of that creek, or you're a frickin hacker. You can't. That's why you're a frickin' hacker."

And that ten thousand times out of ten thousand times, ladies and gents, is what separates the competing professional from plebeians like thee and me.

I suppose my warning is, the draw shot requires a great deal of practice and timing, so perhaps the better way to approach friendly club competition is to eliminate the left side along with the hot bounces of a pull hook and take the far lesser amount of time to ingrain and sustain Hogan's fade. A lot of golfers remember Lee Trevino's adage that "You can talk to a fade but a hook won't listen." Besides, Hogan and Nicklaus and Vijay Singh have done so very well with the power fade weapon.

Undoubtedly, it is probably best that the rest of us keep that controlling left shoulder moving straight up toward the left ear until after the ball is on its way.

It's the point of balance where the left hand is turned into its twist and arch position. It is also the point where the right side (knee, hip, and shoulder) drives under the ball. The left shoulder is thrusting straight up and parallel with the target line.

If the golfer wants a draw, it is at this point that he would turn his left shoulder—along with the left hip and left knee—away from the target line. You can imagine how tight the timing has to be for an intentional draw, and maybe this is why it is so difficult to control—some say it's the most difficult shot in golf. For the amateur, they may be correct.

I overheard Padraig Harrington talking to a colleague about "using golf gloves under both arms" to control his "squat and turn" and "moving onto his left heel with his left hip." I wished for more because it sounded like draw talk to me. But the only other comment was "Nobody does it better than Tiger."

The best controlled hook off the tee I ever saw came from a journeyman pro named Woody Blackburn in the 1985 Crosby at Pebble Beach. The officials had told the young pro out of Pikeville, Kentucky, that he couldn't compete because he hadn't made enough cuts over the past two years to qualify, but luckily, someone got the flu and he was in . . . on the condition that he made the cut or he turned in his playing credentials. Needless to say Woody was worried sick—until he stood on the tee, and then like clockwork he hit this tidy draw that looked like a fishhook. The ball started off down the center, rose with an angle to the right, then turned back down toward the center of the fairway—like a machine—day after day. However, so desperate was he to make the cut and a little money that around the greens and on the putting surface he was a basket case. He would step away from a putt, once, twice, three times—then he'd lick his lips and jab the ball across the slickest greens on the circuit. If Spyglass and Pebble stimped at twelve feet, Cypress stimped at thirteen. Well miraculously, that hook drive held up, and Woody made the final two days. The trouble: Winds off the ocean were gusting up to fifty-five mph and Woody was paralyzed with fear. He had to leave his marker on the ball, and never address it, and backed off so often that he was given a clock warning by the marshal—but this only made him all the more frantic. In spite of his angst, the hook tee shot was somehow maintained. Paul Azinger and I watched him nervously, dreading a train wreck, but no, this story had a happy ending: Woody made it, and collected something like $1,800. But this was not quite the end of the story . . . the man with the trained draw was thus eligible to go on to the Hawaiian Open where he made another $2,600. And then as I checked his progress via the newspaper, he went the next weekend to Riviera and cashed in at $4,800. Each check made him eligible for the next tournament, and he was going to ride that pony to the end of the race—and wouldn't you know, at the next stop, the Izuzu Andy Williams Open in San Diego, Woody shot a fifty-four-hole tournament record of eighteen under par (1968) that wasn't tied until Tiger got hot in 2008. Blackburn, who collected the $72,000 winner's check, played Torrey Pines in San Diego for the next few years until his exemptions ran out. Unfortunately, he never won again.

PHOTO CREDIT: Mike Lilly

Fred Couples hitting a draw down the right side of the twelfth hole at Thousand Oaks. The laid-back, Couples explains that he "just thinks about it" when he wants a draw shot. Of course we must remember that the 1992 Masters winner from Seattle (who put together a sterling performance in the 2010 Masters at age fifty) has been hitting balls for forty years . . . so perhaps he has ingrained a bit of technique along the way.

GREENSIDE SHOTS

Fortunes are made and lost around the green; there is no higher praise than the recognition that "This guy can get up and down from the ball washer."

Sinking a running chip with a right to left roll, or hitting a pitch shot that puts on the brakes on the second bounce . . . so that with a scowl, your miffed opponent hits the gimme back to you—that experience is intoxicating. And so too can be the many challenging lob shots demanded by guardian lakes, bunkers, and creeks.

OUT OF THE ROUGH

Shots from the rough require the golfer to engage the torso to control and power the shot. A hands-and-arm hit will leave you in the long grass—and this advice is true for greenside rough or scooting out from rough under trees. Use your core for strength on shots from the rough.

For a shot across the green to a distant pin, Hogan advocated a "strong" grip instead of the long left thumb and turned his left hand clockwise, so that two or three knuckles of the left hand could be seen. Then came a squeeze of the last three fingers for the left hand—the last two for the right—and a strong torso turn through the ball to a high finish. The ball will roll after landing.

If the flag was closer to him—as in the center of the green—he would use the long left thumb, and then arch and twist the left hand into the ball at impact. The ball will roll less because of the left to right spin.

If the flag was at the near edge of the green, then a "flop" shot much like the bunker "explosion" shot would be in order. The club is opened wide, and strikes an inch behind the ball while the clubface is held open. Then turn through to a high finish.

As a young man, Kevin Riley lived across the street from old Shaughnessy Heights Golf Club years ago in Vancouver. After winning the World Junior Golf Championship in Eugene, Oregon, he turned professional, and went to work for Rod Funseth and Claude Harmon and was soon to become the head professional at Fairmont Country Club in Chatham, New Jersey. Kevin began working for Ben Hogan as a club representative in 1972 and is still working for the company today. One of Kevin's favorite golf stories was a time in 1955 when he observed Mr. Hogan during the pro-am for the Los Angeles Open at Inglewood Country Club. Kevin sat with the famous Lloyd Mangrum, who had served in World War II as a staff sergeant, taking part in both the Normandy Invasion and the Battle of the Bulge. Mangrum came home to Texas with two purple hearts and four battle stars. Recovering from his wounds, he outplayed Bryon Nelson for the U.S. Open in 1946. Together, they watched a shot Hogan made at the par-four eighteenth hole.

The final hole had an elevated green with approximately eight degrees of slope to receive the second shot. Hogan appeared to be in big trouble when his ball took a strange bounce from a sprinkler head and went over the back of the green and down a slight hill. With the gallery watching anxiously, Hogan chipped over the back of the green to a putting surface sloping away from him. The ball took one hop next to

PHOTO CREDIT: Dundee Press

Hogan recovers from Carnoustie rough during his victory in the 1953 British Open.

the hole, at which point it bounced past the cup, then put on the brakes and backed up the eight-degree slope, stopping within two feet of the hole. Kevin had been certain the ball would roll over the front edge of the green for sure, but no, it was another spectacular shot. "That's Hogan," Mangrum concluded. "He does stuff that no one else can."

Hogan advised that he liked to "pick it clean," and Stan Leonard had often called himself "a picker." I had no idea why anyone would want to do that, until he explained Hogan's strategy to me. Hogan wanted to avoid catching any turf or dirt during the shot which could "foul his grooves and diminish the spin to the ball."

SPINNING CHIPS

With faster greens and new rules for the shape of grooves on clubs, it has become more difficult for professional tour players to spin the ball. So where does that leave amateurs?

The controversy of John Daly and Phil Mickelson playing old "square grooves" at Torrey Pines in 2010 highlights the debate. The square grooves on the old Ping Eye 2 club give the ball more spin than the newly sanctioned V-shaped grooves. Manufactured by Karsten Solheim, the Ping Eye 2 wedges were grandfathered following a 2000 court case. As a result, players who still own this wider-grooved club feel that they should still have the advantage of using it.

Other players disagree vigorously; Robert Allenby was pleased with the rule change to the new requirements: "It's changed the game of golf, I think for the better. Now we have to manufacture our way around the golf course."

Veteran Mark Brooks agreed and was quoted in the *Sports Illustrated* 2010 Golf Equipment Issue: "The new grooves have brought back the high, soft shot, the bump-and-run, and everything in between. It's like we're rediscovering our creativity . . . .The old grooves let you be a little sloppy . . . guys got used to playing that low clunker, what I call the controlled chunk. That shot needed to go away. And it has."

Of course that's what Hogan had been saying all along with his emphasis on the need to analyze your next shot and give it your full concentration and study. So wrapped up in the strategy of golf (or manufacture as Allenby would say) was

Hogan that he would not even keep his own score—his caddy did that. Hogan would check the card carefully following the round. He urged amateurs to play "for the joy of the game and hitting good shots as planned." Instead he saw amateurs paralyzing themselves by fixating on the score—"If I bogey in for the last three holes I'll break ninety . . ." This attitude was the "kiss of death," Hogan believed. He wanted the golfer to concentrate on the shot at hand—not on the dumb one two holes ago, but this one . . . right now.

RUNNING CHIP

A long chip with right to left spin will run and will hold its line for better distance control. Strong grip with arched hands. Left shoulder up and the right knee releases on contact.

Right knee chases the ball. Arched hands extend down the line. Left arm and hand roll over in supination while following the ball. The back of the left arched hand is almost facing the ground. The hook effect is moderated because the right elbow remains connected.

BACKSPIN CHIPS

« The back of the left hand is turned to the ground on the takeaway. A chip with backspin will brake and release on the second bounce, "spilling" toward the cup like a putt with not much roll. These are the kind that go in. The grip is weakened by the long left thumb and the elbow dimple to the sky. On grass with a tight lie, the ball is "pinched" between the clubface and the closely mown grass and the ball skids up the club face gathering spin. New groove regulations are putting this shot into the "specialty" category.

The ball is "nipped" before » any contact with the ground by an opened blade and a connected shoulder tilt. Hands are held in the Hogan mold. The back of the left hand looks to the target for an abbreviated follow-through.

UP-AND-OVER FLOP SHOT

① Weight distribution at address is fifty-fifty. Open blade, strong grip with left palm to the ground to reduce the clutching effect of rough. Aim one inch behind the ball.

② Shoulder controls the takeaway. Wrist hinging. Hands in front of chest.

③ Blade held open through impact. Left palm down. The right hand holds its angle; notice that the club shaft therefore is a straight- line extension of the left arm, and not the right, which would mean a breakdown of the left wrist.

④ The golfer's hands are turned to a "strong grip" at address to anticipate the deep rough clutching the hosel and turning the toe of the club over. Stay crouched and hold the clubface open through the ball at impact.

BACKSPIN LOBS

⑤ The clubface is open. At address the ball position is centered between the feet.

⑥ The wrists hinge to ninety degrees right from the address in a steep takeaway.

⑦ Hands are well in front of the ball at impact to pinch the ball between the ground and the clubface.

PHOTO CREDIT: Linda Leonard

⑧ The face is held open so that the ball can "skid" up the face of the grooves to increase backspin. The angle of the right hand is held constant so that the left wrist does not break down.

⑨ The magical device is in control of the shot with strong connection to the rotating torso. The shaft is an extension of the left arm.

CHAPTER 16

PROBLEM SHOTS

Hogan always made a quick evaluation of the lie as he approached the ball. These few seconds gave him the complete picture of the task before him; he believed that the analysis should begin before the golfer gets to the bag and selects the club. Basically, he checked distance and wind but then he asked:

Where is the best place I can get up and down?
Where must I land the ball for a run at the pin?
What will the ball do if I hit that spot?

Bruce Chambers was a club-fitter from New Zealand who remembers his first glimpse of Ben Hogan during the 1961 U.S. Open in Bloomfield, Michigan. Although won by Gene Littler, Chambers was struck by Hogan's impeccable strategy. It became apparent to Chambers that Hogan took much care in the placement of each shot in order to increase the opportunity for a birdie chance on the next.

At the par four eighth hole on the South Course—475 yards—designed by the master architect Donald Ross, Hogan was playing with Bruce Crampton, the young Australian up-and-comer.

After their drives Crampton was away by two yards, and ripped a long five iron boldly onto the green. Chambers saw Hogan shaking his head and wondered why. Then he was surprised to watch Hogan lay up between two bunkers, but then he realized what the determined strategist was doing. Hogan had won the Open on this same course ten years earlier, and as the best wedge player in the game, he put his third shot two feet from the pin assuring him of a par. Crampton was at the mercy of a treacherous green and three putted for bogie.

We all get a little absentminded when playing golf, and sometimes we overlook a potential problem and ignore it . . . to our regret.

The best example of this management strategy that I have seen was given by perhaps a young Hogan in the making: Jackson Rue was eight when I first met him at an executive par three course. After introductions, his father went to the pro shop and Jackson was on the practice range hitting his driver while I watched. "Can you hit the 150 yard sign?" I asked.

"Yes," came the quiet answer, "but it's the wrong club."

"Oh that doesn't matter," I said, and watched him shrug before he rolled it four feet to the side of the marker. He gave me a glance for my reaction.

I asked again, "Can you actually hit the sign with the ball?"

Eight-year-old Jackson nodded, swung again and bounced one off the 150 marker. "Good," I said. "Can you hit the 125 sign?"

"Yes, but it's the wrong club."

"That's OK," I said.

He nodded, and bounced the next shot off the sign.

This was the kind of imagination that Hogan liked to use during practice—but we were talking about taking in the context of the next shot while approaching the ball, and Jackson was good at that too, as I found out the next day.

We teed off at the twelfth hole near Point Grey's clubhouse because Jackson's father was not sure if his son could play a regulation eighteen holes. They had always played executive

Another Ben Hogan perhaps? Eight-year-old Jackson Rue with South African touring pro Doug McGuigan waiting to tee it up.

courses. Jackson even had some course records on the par three tracks. He had also registered six holes in one, and was quick to tell me that Tiger, at that age, had only four.

Jackson hit his driver with an athletic swing learned by watching the Golf Channel, and put it out there a solid 170 yards. He then fell into step with me as we walked down the hill toward his ball—his father as caddy bringing up the rear. It was then Jackson turned on his Ben Hogan mode, and blew me away. This eight-year-old kid, who would take four shots to hit the green on this five hundred yard hole he'd never seen before, who had not even reached his drive yet, said something quite new to me, that distance from a far-away green: "Oh, oh," he said in a concerned voice, "They've got the pin really tucked today." Following his 170 yard drive with two fairway clubs, he hit a wedge from an angle chosen in order to avoid a bunker, and then sank the four-foot putt for his par. Hogan might have liked that display.

UPHILL LIE

For an uphill shot, stand farther from the ball in a ready position where you sit on a barstool in balance with the hill. Grip down on the club and don't let the swing pull you off balance.

Swing through following the slope of the hill.

DOWNHILL LIE

Weight on front foot in a ready position for address. Grip down on the handle.

Swing with the slope of the hill to a full extension of the arms. The hips do not move toward the target.

BALL ABOVE THE FEET

Grip down on the handle. The ball will fly to the left so adjust your target line accordingly. The slope will increase the loft, so that a seven iron will become an eight. Take a lower number: a six.

BALL BELOW THE FEET

Stand closer for the ready position. In a normal stance you are likely to lose your balance down the hill.

CADDY SHOTS

Older golfers who remember their caddy days of hanging around waiting for a loop will also recall the competitions that arose with the risk of small change. It was then that future golfers learned "under the gun" how to open a wedge to the right angle to hit the golf ball over the top of a tree from a position closest to the base of the tree. Chipping to a metal push-in sign to sound a bong was another way to win a nickel. But perhaps the hardest, was swinging a right-handed club from a left-handed position to sound the bong.

Canadian professional Dave Barr probably benefited most from such "crazy" practices. During his time on tour he won twice, but more emphatically he finished in the top ten over forty times—the most spectacular moment being his second place finish in the 1985 U.S. Open. At the 1994 Greater Hartford Open in Cromwell, Connecticut, Barr was caught in an impossible position much to the interest of television announcer Ken Venturi, the great amateur who challenged Hogan at Cypress Point.

Barr was tied at the end of seventy-two holes with Joey Sindelar and Mark Brooks. On the second play-off hole, Barr watched his eight iron second shot spin back toward a greenside lake, coming to rest on the top of a railroad tie which was the popular banking method of course architect Peter Dye. With nowhere to stand, Barr remembered something from his days as a kid "trying to make some fun out of practice." He turned his sand wedge over, and calmly hit it with a left-handed swing onto the green—four feet from the cup. Venturi was very impressed with Barr's creativity . . . even though when the dust had settled, his par lost to a lengthy Mark Brooks putt for birdie.

Anthony Kim was caught in a similar predicament at the 2010 Phoenix Open and salvaged his par. Phil Mickelson had to backhand his second shot on the first hole at the 2009 Masters and still made par. Since then, my first few shots at the driving range are seven iron chips from the lefty side.

Once you have become fairly good with the fundamental swing techniques Hogan used, there are a few variations worth considering:

1. For short chips you might find sharper success by opening the stance line left of the target for the feet, knees, and hips at address. The shoulders are held parallel to the target line and are in full control. You might want to keep Hogan's "closed" stance for longer shots—but you may find—following a period of trial—more direction control with an open stance for short shots.
2. For putts on fast greens you may find that gripping down on the handle of the club will lighten the feel, and give you more distance control for very fast greens. For slow greens the full grip will give you a longer lever to swing, and more distance will result.
3. The same effect will prove useful on chips to fast greens: full grip for slow greens; grip down for fast.
4. Gripping down the handle for a long shot will translate into five yards per half inch.
5. Try controlling distance with your driver by gripping down and/or using half swings and

Take an eight iron and turn it over on the toe. Connect the triangle and with your right shoulder tilt down, then up. The speed of your turning body dictates the distance.

three-quarter swings for uncommon shots "under the wind" or for low left-to-right shots from under trees.

BUNKERS

Finding descriptions of Ben Hogan's technique for bunker shots had some difficulties attached to the search. For example, several caddies I spoke to could not remember Mr. Hogan ever being in a trap. Further, a review of Hogan literature turns up many volumes on his ball-striking and all kinds of theory about "his secret," but virtually nothing on bunker play. Hogan himself wrote precious little on the subject of bunkers, except for a pre-accident book from 1948 titled *Power Golf*. In this small tome there were some pictures of blurred hands and shafts bent wildly under the stress of the swing, but little in the way of detailed analysis. Hogan's only encouragement was in the title for the section where he insisted: "Bunker Shots Are Easy." He claimed they were easy because, "You don't even have to hit the ball on a short bunker shot." The other reason cited was because of the sand wedge "invented" by Gene Sarazen, who introduced his prototype with victories in the 1932 U.S. and British Opens. Hogan said:

"This is one of the easiest shots in golf, but most beginners are terrified at the idea of having to play out of a bunker. I can't understand why they should be, because it is a shot which allows more of a margin or error than any other." However encouraging as this insight was meant to be, Hogan gave little more instruction other than "Explode the short shots and pick the long ones clean."

Joey Sindelar shared Hogan's attitude that bunker shots were easy. I found this out during a practice round at Spyglass Hill at the 1985 Crosby (now named the AT&T Pebble Beach National Pro-Am even though Bob Hope begged them to call it the Bing Crosby National Pro-Am presented by AT&T. But times had changed—the economy was different, and old loyalties were gone.)

Anyway, I was playing the first—a 600 yard hole with a sharp dogleg left—when I saw another single player with his caddy up on a high shelf about 300 yards from the well-bunkered green. I'll wait for him, I thought, and practiced putting expecting him to play up with his second shot. Well, he didn't—and it quickly became obvious that he was waiting for me, because he was going for what looked like a green hole in a donut made of white sand.

The controlling influence of the triangle is evident. Hands remain in their mold established at address. This professional shows us the different angles for the stance line and the target line. The club's shaft moves parallel to the stance line and so on the way down will cut across the target line to the ball from the outfield to the infield.

Sindelar's driver from the fairway 306 yards away finished pin high in a bunker. "I like traps. No bad bounces," explained this resident of Rochester who, every New York winter, would beat on an old car tire in his garage with a driver as a strength exercise.

It was really Stan Leonard who took the time to show me Hogan's technique for traps. Stan was head pro at Marine Drive Golf Club, and during November he coached the University of BC's golf team before heading to Desert Island Club in Palm Springs for a winter break. One bleak day nobody else showed up, so I took advantage while Stan demonstrated the stance, the setup, and position of the hands that Hogan used.

SAND PLAY DETAILS

- Wiggle your feet into the sand to feel the texture, and to establish a steady base that won't allow slippage.
- Open the stance with most of your weight on the left foot—this will mark the low point of the swing's arc.
- Check the connection of the magical device: Left armpit on the rib cage; right elbow on the hip.
- The grip is held in a constant mold throughout the shot, with the left and right hands in dorsiflexion. At address, the hands are well ahead of the ball so that the wrists are already partially hinged.
- The club's face is open, and hovering just one inch behind the ball.
- When the hands are as far back as the shot requires for distance, the left shoulder triggers the triangle to return on the "outside to inside" track to enter the sand behind the ball.

Knees are flexed. Right knee "kicked in slightly" to a position where they both remain steady. As the left shoulder pushes down, the wrists hinge fully, and rise quickly in a V-shaped swing. On takeaway, the open blade cuts across the target line because the shoulder plane follows the stance line, which is open. »

Hold the left palm down as the open clubface slides with steady tempo under the ball so that it leaves the trap on a bed of sand. The golfer's chest turns toward the flag with the molded hands in position between the shoulders. The right knee is pulled by the rising left shoulder toward the stable and flexed left knee. By the way—this was his first shot and in it went.

- Hogan's last word on the subject of bunkers was: "While hitting through the sand and on to the finish, make sure that the hands never turn over, or pronate. Keep the face of the club open." This statement would logically obviate the need to apply the secret—better to keep it simple with hands held firmly in one position throughout the shot anyway. Professionals prefer "the left palm down" all the way.

PHOTO CREDIT: Associated Press

Hogan in bunker with the hands, shoulder, and arm triangle in strong position.

CHAPTER 17

GOLF EXERCISES AT HOME

The balance, posture, and poise Hogan demonstrated are important characteristics of any athletic activity. These characteristics are particularly noticeable in good golfers, skiers, and ballroom dancers.

Where as the average Saturday night shuffler gets on the dance floor and pumps his arms up and down as if he is getting water from an old fashioned well, the experienced ballroom dancer—and of course the professional golfer—moves his body and arms in one smooth and beautifully coordinated flow of motion.

Although the arms seem to be the natural levers for these activities, the body has the strength, power, and coordination to do the job much better. Use the torso, and start looking like a professional.

Ben Hogan virtually "invented practice" even though during his time on the Gold Trail, players were more enamored of the good life featuring fast friends and smooth whiskey. Walter Hagen, five-time PGA champion, began far more often with a hangover than with a pre-game warm-up at the driving range. And if Jimmy Demaret ever saw Hogan hitting balls after a match to iron out some swing kinks, he'd shake his head at all the time wasted . . . one could be at the bar explaining the vagaries of golf to attentive young ladies interested in the high life on the Gold Trail.

PHOTO CREDIT: Tim Mah

Golf at its higher levels must be considered as one of the performing arts. Top professionals playing the game demonstrate the grace of a body in motion.

Julius Boros, two-time U.S. Open Champion, enjoyed life at the table and—although a trifle overweight—moved placidly through his career with the likes of Ed "Porky" Oliver, who played golf every day but hit only a few warm-up shots from a shag bag. I'm sure they would never believe Tiger's daily routine which includes a cardio vascular regime, free-standing weights, machines, pulleys, and his own exercises of stretching and swinging with weights.

The PGA sends a gymnasium and weight training van to all tournaments, and others follow Tiger in a movement which produces some amazing young athletes—like "Spiderman" Camilo Villegas—who make puny some of the ordinary golf courses whose length is no longer a factor, as these Elysian Fields are bombarded by a lethal combination of weight training and equipment technology.

If you are heading for competition you will be best advised to begin a serious study of daily exercise. Personal trainers and weight-training gymnasia, with modern injury-preventing machinery, abound. And if you are now—or intend to be—a senior golfer, get into the habit of daily exercise.

EXERCISES FOR THE WORKING AMATEUR

Ben Hogan practiced every day. After all, he was a professional, and had the time for it . . . but more than that, he loved the focus of the mind, and the isolation. Hitting balls was, no doubt, his shelter against the world . . . shutting it out, forgetting the demons, and dependent upon no one but himself.

Hogan admitted to his biographers James Dodson and Curt Sampson that "I couldn't wait for the sun to come up the next morning so that I could get out on the course again."

Tiger Woods has a regimen of which Hogan would probably have approved, although he was never one for weight training. Hogan believed strongly in the importance of putting those shiny dime marks on his irons. Tiger's daily regimen when not competing looks like this:

- Up at 6:00 AM for weight training (90 minutes)
- Breakfast (30 minutes)
- Practice fairway (2 hours)
- Putting green (30 minutes)
- Play nine holes (1 hour)
- Lunch (1 hour)
- Practice tee (2 hours)
- Short game area (1 hour)

The Crunch. Knees bent. Hands across chest. Crunch up and hold it for a count of five. Work to increase the count so that you can watch a thirty-second television advertisement while in the curl and hold position.

Planking (or bridging) is another good abdominal exercise. A substitute for push-ups, it is also called "the anti-rotational core workout."

- Play nine holes (1 hour)
- Putting green (30 minutes)
- Home at 5:30 PM

Now, you might envy this regime because it represents an atmosphere that is set aside and paid for by the very skills it is designed to sharpen. However, I'm betting that a different set of circumstances confronts you every morning and you have to go to a different kind of job.

The question is then, how do you continue your regimented life which supports your family and lifestyle—but still maintain or develop a decent golf game?

Well, here are some strength and flexibility exercises you can do at home and which will serve you well in support of your version of Ben Hogan's system.

Lee Trevino advised amateur golfers that they should "hit three hundred balls a day to improve your game." Well we've been through that idea—and might agree with man who won the Canadian Open, the U.S. Open, and the British Open in his impressive season of 1971—but circumstances might not allow us to follow that formula. Though three hundred balls might be impossible to work in to your day, three hundred abdominal crunches are not. And at a rate of forty per minute you could have them all done in the privacy of your home in just nine minutes.

The beauty of crunches at home is that you don't have to travel . . . and you don't have to do them all at once. You should do your exercises in three sets with a rest—or a different activity—in between. When you watch television, wait for the ads then with your feet flat on the floor (or couch) with knees bent—then crunch up halfway, and watch the ad from between your knees. Ads are usually thirty seconds long—you can stretch yourself by crunching half-way up for the length of a one-minute commercial.

One of my favorite weekend warriors is Paul Nemath, former wrestling coach at the University of BC and a technical advisor to Nike in Beaverton, Oregon.

The body is held straight from the head to the ankles supported by the upper arm. Keep the shoulder square. Hold the position for ten seconds . . . rest ten seconds. Repeat for a set of three.

Nemeth brought this idea home for me when I met him at a sports banquet and playfully set up with him in the Olympic "ready wrestle" position. His wife jumped in because of concern for Paul's ninety-one years—but not before I could feel the strength in his shoulders, neck, arms, and back.

"What do you do for a work-out?" I asked.

"I do one push-up a day," he said very pleased with himself. Then, seeing the confusion on my face added with a grin, "One for every year of my life."

"I get up and do thirty push-ups—then I brush my teeth. Then I do thirty more—and then I shave. Next I do thirty-one. Then I shower and go down to breakfast. A good start to the day. As we say at Nike—just do it!"

You might not be in tune with push-ups because of shoulder problems perhaps, but there is a good substitute: planking—an exercise which focuses on the core muscles and strengthening the torso.

Begin with a straight frame held motionless by contracted muscles of the entire body for a count of ten. Quantity is not as important as your form. The muscles stiffen as if in preparation for a punch to the abdomen, or when bracing for impact on a long golf shot. A moderate daily workout would be three sets of thirty seconds each.

Planking can be made more challenging by extending the arms in push-up position, or by raising one leg or one hand. But really, achieving the proper form that will engage core muscles to connect the front and back, the legs and shoulders, will develop the necessary fitness for a good torso swing.

And speaking of necessary fitness, it is essential that part of your daily routine includes stretching exercise for the shoulders. Tendons and ligaments get short and stiff unless attended to regularly (read: daily).

For posture, back up to the wall and press both elbows against the surface in a pulsating motion ten times; rest, then continue for a set of three.

For a greater challenge extend the arms fully and press for another set of three.

Back in the gymnasium you can increase the stretch by turning two small dumbbells from a position parallel to the floor, to trying to touch the back of your hands against the wall. Hold the stretch for twenty to thirty seconds.

More for the core. With a medicine ball of medium weight, sweep back through the half golf swing and then through. Keep your knees flexed.

Strengthen your hand control beginning with light dumbbells and working to medium weight, while applying Hogan's secret move through an imagined ball. Stay strongly connected at the elbows as you turn the lower body slowly through the impact zone.

« Lunges are great for a leg stretch as well as a workout for the thighs. You can cover ground down a hallway, outside on a field, or standing on one spot. Good posture, with head held high and a straight back, promotes good balance. Fingertips on the wall are fine for safety.

Most golfers stop at the kiosk after nine. To get back into the game, here is a good stretch for the tenth tee. Put both hands behind your head and pull the elbows back to touch an imaginary wall behind you. Hold for twenty to thirty seconds and feel the tendons pull out in a relaxing stretch. »

If your back is a little tight—put your left foot up on a bench and let your left arm reach down for thirty seconds; feel the nice stretch for your right side back. Repeat with the other foot up.

Wringing a towel is a good way to work on feel as well as strengthen the grip for impact. Both hands twist and arch with palmar flexion. You can even do this one on the steering wheel of your car.

Davis Love III emphasized the need for stretching during a match and has four or five exercises to use on the course. He does lunges with one hand on a golf cart or ball washer. In chilly weather, he stretches his hamstrings by putting the heel of one leg waist high on the back of a cart or bench, and with the other knee slightly flexed, lets the large muscles at the back of his thigh stretch out over twenty or thirty seconds without any bouncing. Shoulder stretches are attended to anywhere on the course, and as often as needed.

CHAPTER 18

HOGAN'S FUNDAMENTALS

When I first described the Magical Device, I assumed that everyone would be clearly aware of Mr. Hogan's elaborate preparatory moves to position himself properly before putting his precise and distinct swing into action. However, like most assumptions, it was, no doubt, wrong, so here is a brief review of the content of *Five Lessons* and *Life* magazine's August 8, 1955, issue; both sources were designed primarily for the full shot with long-shafted clubs.

Those who read Hogan's *Five Lessons* devoured the details of insights Hogan presented in his deliberate and detailed way, shared them in lengthy discussions with friends, and will recognize these basic concepts. This is not to say that everyone should adopt these techniques. In the present book, we have dealt with the task of understanding ten key positions which explains, in detail, the short game from 120 yards and in.

The concentration for this book has focused on Hogan's short game system, which relies on the development of a torso powered golf swing; using the Magical Device for direction control; and the application of Hogan's Secret for distance. If however, there are helpful pieces or reminders in this review of Hogan's fundamentals—so much the better. Whether you use some of them or none of them is up to you, but chances are you should at least be aware of them, and therefore understand why you are not using this technique or that.

Hogan believed that "the average golfer is entirely capable of building a repeating swing and breaking eighty, if he learns to perform a small number of correct movements, and conversely it follows, eliminating a lot of movements which tend to keep the swing from repeating."

Such as:

- A nervous, fidgety waggle without a purpose directly related to the next swing.
- Re-gripping repeatedly.
- Moving the bottom of the arc by swaying.
- Straightening either knee during the swing before completely clear of the impact zone.

STANCE

Hogan set his stance with great care. The ball was positioned exactly one inch inside his left heel for all shots and this platform reflected his pursuit of a steady foundation for every swing. The right foot was almost square to the target line. For full shots with long-shafted clubs, the left foot angled toward the target in a closed position. The right knee was rock-steady in its place with the weight on the inside edge of the foot—and never on the outside edge or the little toe. The same inside edge pressure was needed for the left foot, where the weight was focused on the base of the big toe.

The right shoulder was lowered because the elbow rests on the crest of the pelvis, ready to act as a fulcrum. The shoulders were square to the target line, and the armpits were connected to the rib cage.

Hogan used a wide stance for the driver but adjusted his stance according to the length of the shaft and the distance required for the shot by moving his right foot. The ball was aligned off the left heel for consistent trajectory, and the right foot came closer to the target line if he used a short-shafted club.

GRIP

Hogan was very precise about his grip. It began with a "long left thumb" when he was to call on his power fade or left to right spin for stopping the ball.

Hogan held the club in the palm of his left hand running from the pad at the base of the palm to the pad at the base of his forefinger.

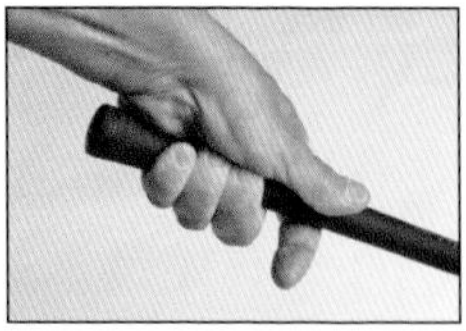

The last three fingers squeeze stability into the left hand structure. Snead said that he "wanted to squeeze the juice out of it."

Hogan didn't argue. "You have to hold on to the club for a hard hit, don't you?" he answered when asked about the importance of a firm versus light grip.

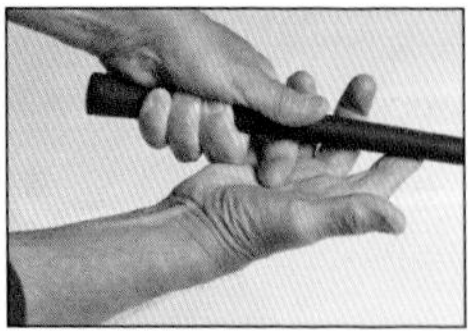

The forearms stay "soft" so that stiffness does not impair rhythm. There is a familiar strength in the hands, which allows shoulders and arms to be held in a relaxed anticipation of coming effort, but the strength is there.

The little finger of the right hand fits around the groove offered by the forefinger and thumb of the left hand. The two central fingers of the right hand close the left thumb snugly into the palm of the right hand. The thumb and forefinger of the right hand fit high on top, in a softer grasp. A squeeze of the controlling last three fingers of the left hand and the middle two fingers of the right hand unite the hands into a strong unit.

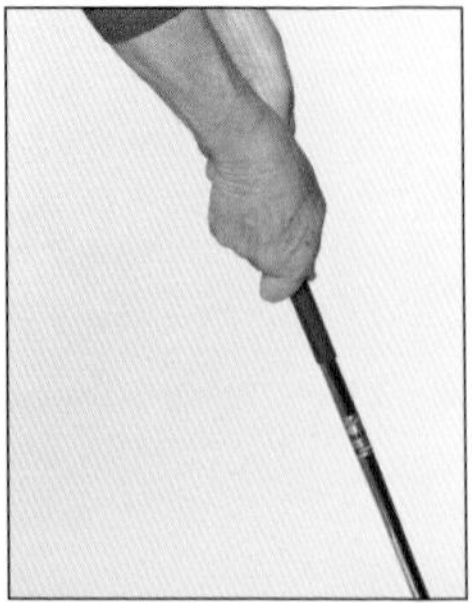

Completed grip

PLANE

Hogan's vision of his swing plane to the top of his backswing was illustrated in Ravielli's famous drawing, in which Hogan imagines his head poking out through a hole in a pane of glass angling down squarely to the target line. Here is Bill McLuckie's version of it.

To continue talking about the swing plane for just a moment, many of you will know that Hogan changed the square glass image as he came down into the ball by turning his back on the target, and raising his left shoulder to bring the hands into position for their ride on the Magical Device to impact. The shoulders changed from their parallel position to the target line, and turned into a slightly closed position.

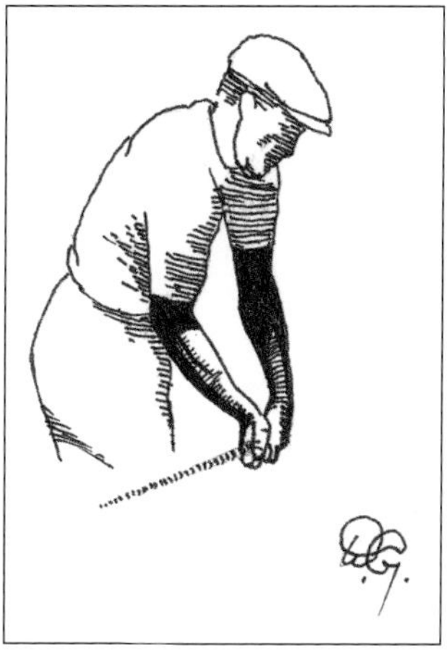

SWING TO THE FINISH

Hogan's finish reflected the continuous balance shown throughout the swing from the address to the top of the backswing, through impact, and then to the follow-through. Once again, the completed swing should reflect the balance Hogan strived for on every shot. The old pros used to say, "Pose for the photograph—two seconds."

A LAST WORD

If you train yourself to do just three things repeatedly without having to think about them while you swing to the target, you will shock your opponents and they will pay homage to your diligence by handing you money on a regular basis:

1. Start the downswing just before the hands stretch to the top, by moving the left knee over top of the left foot which settles you into the barstool position—from whence the real action starts. (I would venture a guess that almost all double-digit golfers omit this crucial move.)
2. Follow that move of the left knee with an upward thrust of the left shoulder and the strongly connected Magical Device brings the clubhead to the ball powered by the torso.
3. Imagine that the left shoulder is attached to your right knee so that they move together, along with the right hip and shoulder under the ball through impact.

If, as Tom Watson predicts, "you destroy a good swing a millimeter at a time" by trying to get more out of it, you'll need to recognize where you slowly went wrong and review the part out of kilter.

You'll know how to re-train it—if you've had the patience to learn Hogan's system. Questions? Email tedhunt@shaw.ca.

PHOTO CREDIT: Jay Hebert

And this is where you'll wind up.

THE NINETEENTH HOLE

MORE STORIES WITH A HOGAN TWIST

THE INDELIBLE STAIN OF POVERTY

"Mr. Hogan was not a chatty guy." This characterization was admitted seriously by a succinct man who caddied for "the Hawk" around the Texas courses near Fort Worth. "He was always lookin' at the next shot, and didn't want to be disturbed . . . this was his business. But don't get me wrong . . . if the caddy does his job . . . then Mr. Hogan does anything for you when the game was done. A lot of Hollywood guys were like that—Crosby, Hope, Sean Connery. They've been tapped-out before. Like us."

Of course Hogan knew this point to be true because he had begun caddying at age eleven following his father's suicide. He had to help put food on the table at sixty-five cents per round at time when a dime tip was a big score.

Bob Hope tried to make a living in burlesque and prize fighting, under the name of Packy East. Bing Crosby saw the opportunity for his first job in Hollywood crushed when a charge of drinking while driving on Sunset Boulevard made him miss an audition the following morning—and it looked like he was finished. Sean Connery was born on the east side of Edinburgh in an apartment block with one toilet for twelve families. He slept in the bottom drawer of his mother's bureau until baby brother Charles put him out of that and onto the kitchen floor. Like Hogan, Connery quit school early to sell newspapers and deliver milk. So all these men understood Ben Hogan. They knew where his neurotic determination came from—and they recognized a man who was polishing a talent.

Hogan first met Bing Crosby at the crooner's pro-am which began in Rancho Santa Fe in 1937. Hogan was trying to escape the torment of mind-searing hooks. He won eighty-five dollars in that first year of the Crosby Clambake, a golf week which tried to bring a little sparkle back into Depression-era life and help local charities at the same time. (His arch-rival Sam Snead picked up the five hundred dollar first place check signed by Crosby. Sam looked it over and said, "If you don't mind Mr. Crosby, I'd rather have cash.")

Even though Hogan was struggling with his game, Crosby saw something in the young professional and offered Hogan a chance to come along with him and

PHOTO CREDIT: First Cut Golf

Hogan hitting a nine iron punch shot to win his first individual tour victory at Pinehurst, North Carolina, in 1940. Hogan's caddy appears to have absorbed "the Hawk's" instructions for caddies: "Stay in front, or behind me—out of sight" and "Don't touch the club's face or grip. Hand it to me by the shaft. I don't want any sweat or skin oil on 'em."

the effusive Bob Hope on a series of exhibitions to South America designed to introduce the game to growing communities. At first Hogan was skeptical about teaming up with these two extroverted comedians who were soon to spread zany American comedy around the world with their famous series of "Road" movies. (It began with *The Road to Singapore* and then on to another six destinations before they were through; it seemed that every glamorous city in the world had a road to it, and Bing Crosby and Bob Hope were on it.)

PHOTO CREDIT: Associated Press

Bing Crosby and Hogan at the Clambake in Pebble Beach.

Hogan did not approve of the outrageous antics on the screen . . . but he saw something else in these two famous partners; they both loved golf and were completely focused, once on the course. They were serious . . . and very respectful of Ben's business-like approach to the game—his business. He found also that they admired not only his talent but also the good manners taught to him by his mother. So it was considered a great compliment to play with these two comics and, in fact, he accepted the offer to travel with them to South America for a series of exhibitions designed to increase the game's popularity.

Of course there would be—inevitably—minor breakdowns in behavior, as one caddy revealed: "Mr. Crosby was a true four handicap. Mr. Hope was more like a seven and had to work hard to beat Bing. One day when Hope had beaten him, Mr. Crosby said he'd left his wallet at home so he couldn't pay. A few days later Bing was paying for something in the pro shop and was handed change—but Mr. Hope snatched the bills out of the clerk's hand and ran like hell."

But there was no doubt that these two studied their golf. On the movie set, Crosby would leave for the practice range at Bel-Air Club, ten minutes away.

Hope had a net installed for his use on the set, remembering that "One day I damned near killed a cameraman."

On one of their 1945 exhibition matches at the Tanta Anito course, it was noted in the *Evening Independent* newspaper that Hope and Crosby had scores of seventy-three, while Babe Didrickson had a seventy-one. "Lieutenant Ben Hogan, an air force pilot and former Texas pro, had 33–34 for a tidy 67."

Crosby and Hope must have enjoyed Hogan's example because five years later Crosby played in the British Amateur in Scotland. The following year at the encouragement of his Texan friend, Bing played the British Amateur in Wales.

They even made a little golf movie together called *Faith Hope and Hogan*.

A CADDY LOOKS BACK FONDLY

There's a nice passage about Ben Hogan from the book *Beyond Xs and Os* by Tom Berthel and longtime University of Iowa football coach Hayden Fry. This College Hall of Fame football giant was born in Eastland, Texas, during the Great Depression and never forgot his time with Hogan.

Coach Fry writes:

> "When I wasn't busy at the store, I caddied at the country club and learned quickly that golf is chock full of life lessons (especially with a handicap like mine). One of my favorite memories of caddying came in 1940. I was eleven years old and the Odessa Country Club was hosting a big tournament. One of the players came over from Fort Worth but his caddy got sick and was unable to make the trip, so they asked me to carry the guy's bag. We walked three rounds together, one round each day for three consecutive days. He was a real nice guy and in three rounds of golf he never said a word to me, never asked me about the yardage or anything else. (Being as young as I was I guess I didn't blame him. I didn't know anything anyway.) After the final round on the third day, he shook my hand, said "thank you," and handed me a twenty dollar bill. Twenty dollars . . . I couldn't believe it. In those days, we earned a dollar for carrying a bag eighteen holes, which was real good money. Turns out, the guy's name was Ben Hogan. I

wrapped my fist around that money and went straight home to show mom and daddy (a little concerned they'd think I stole it). We hadn't seen many twenty dollar bills.

I followed Mr. Hogan's career pretty closely after that and have never forgotten the lesson he taught me that week: If you don't have something important to say, keep your mouth shut."

The world is blocked out for a moment while these two plot the next challenge: Hogan's short-cut at Cypress Point.

THE LAST WORD IS SOMETIMES CRUSHING

Ben Hogan loved a good caddy story. And, although polite and socially astute himself, if the anecdote were to be laced with salty language—so much the better. His favorite was one told by Sean Connery:

"I was filming in Edinburgh but there was to be a delay, and so I was invited to compete in the Scottish Amateur Match Play in the Highlands—way the hell-and-gone up north in Dornoch. Well I'm hardly prepared, but I phone a friend in Dornoch, and ask him to get me a good caddy because I won't know the course. He says he'll do that, so when I arrive there's this fella waiting for me at the locker room entrance. He's a wee small man . . . indeterminable age . . . wearing a World War Two army great coat. The collar's turned up against the drizzle and he's got this safety pin holding the top of the collar closed across the bridge of his nose. Sticking out under the safety pin is the stub of a rolled cigarette. And there's these two grey eyes peering out from under a cloth cap as he touches the brim to acknowledge my presence—but he never say a God-damned word. Independent bugger. Doesn't speak for three fucking days. When I ask for a five iron, he'd just shake his head and tap the four. In three days—not a word! No 'Well done, sir' or 'Good shot.' Nothing!"

"I'd been winning all my matches with some pretty fair golf through those whistling Highland gales. The countryside was nothing but wind, gorse, and slanting rain. On the final day I was doing not too badly through some filthy weather and we come to the eighteenth, a nasty, 456 yard par four into a gale off Dornoch Firth. I hit the drive on all six screws, then I slash a three wood under the wind to ten feet from the pin, and this little bastard says nothing. Just stands there with the wet dripping off his shoulders, the cigarette stub still sticking out under the safety pin as he puts away the three wood. Well, I glower at him but still he says nothing. That was a good shot, I declare, my tone demanding a response.

'Aye,' he says slowly. 'And we've been waiting a rather long time for it haven't we?'"

Connery really didn't begin to play golf until forced to take lessons in order to prepare for his third outing as James Bond in the 007 thriller *Goldfinger*. As a sidelight: When he was taking his first halting steps as a beginner, Sean was in the locker room at Bel-Air getting ready for his second lesson. A member dressed only in socks, a jock, and a cap, stood swaying before Sean with a third martini is his hand. "Fuggit," said the drunk. "Jus . . . just fuggit . . . that's all I have to say—fuggit!"

It's amazing that after such a negative example Connery worked his way to a single-digit handicap and played in some elite professional company.

Connery takes a few swings in the Bond film, but the scene that captured a lot of laughs occurred when, one-up on the seventeenth hole at Stoke Park Club in England, Goldfinger loses a ball off the fairway in eight inch rough. Bond is poking around with a club, while his caddy notes: "You'll win if he doesn't find his ball."

"He won't," declares the worldly James Bond. "I'm standing on it."

Of course this scene caused great delight at the time, but it was far from Sean Connery, who was every bit as conscientious as Hogan. Both were sticklers for the laws of the game and both would stare down anyone trying to bend them.

THE IRISH CADDY

Liam Higgens was just a lad from the Waterville Athletic Club who could hit the ball a mile. He had been invited to New York for a long drive competition, and with his first shot had driven over the 380 yard first hole at Westchester where his ball plugged. His competition withdrew.

The next day he was invited to play with Ben Hogan, Bing Crosby, Bob Hope, and Claude Harmon, the 1948 Masters Champion.

Playing the third hole at Westchester Liam struck a one iron from a downhill lie to within a few feet of the pin. Hogan, who had won the U.S. Open with Merion with his own famous one iron to the final green, said generously, "That's the best shot I've ever seen. What was the yardage?"

"Don't know," said young Liam, "we don't play by yardage in Ireland. We look at the target and hit the ball. Besides, I've never played here before."

CARNOUSTIE: HOGAN'S ONLY BRITISH OPEN

The claustrophobic sixth hole at Carnoustie was 565 yards long, with bunkers that could house a Volkswagen. They were placed near the landing area to catch any misaligned drives, with another set of bunkers waiting for the second shot as well. While most players, like former British Open champion Bob Locke, hit four iron, seven iron to lay up, Ben Hogan hit full driver down a narrow strip of brown grass running between out-of-bounds on the left and the fairway to the right which was pock-marked with bunkers. He ignored the main fairway altogether, then hit his spoon to the green over more traps and a twisting burn. This he did each day with two-putt birdies for each round to win the Open by six strokes. Members of Carnoustie, who came to love the "Wee Ice Mon," refer to this pathway as "Hogan's Alley."

To honor Hogan's audacious performance on the fiftieth anniversary of the feat, the Carnoustie Golf Club arranged a long-drive contest on the same hole. The sixth, once called simply "Long" was usually into prevailing winds which can really toughen up this already well fortified test of golf. Champion golfers Vijay Singh, Colin Montgomerie, Ian Woosnam, Paul Lawrie, Adam Scott, and Sam Torrence were invited to play the hole using clubs and balls from the Hogan

PHOTO CREDIT: Associated Press

Ben Hogan drives at the sixth hole at Carnoustie, 1953. Caddy Cecil Timms almost drove the Hawk crazy with constant smiles and chatter. Worse, he would cover his eyes when Hogan putted. Hogan, however, was in complete control as one can see by his hands still grasping the club with his characteristic molded grip. Hogan was heard to say, "Timmy, shut your mouth and stand still."

era—1953. The winning drive was Arjun Atwal at 251 yards. Paul Lawrie—Open Champion after catching the ill-fated Jean Van de Velde in 1999—was second with 245 yards. Vijay Singh rapped it out there 219 yards, and Colin Montgomerie was not the shortest professional with 203 yards. Just a bit different with today's equipment. The plaque placed at the hole reads:

BEN HOGAN—OPEN CHAMPION—1953

In each of the four rounds of the 1953 Open Championship, Hogan chose the tight driving line between fairway bunkers and the out of bounds fence. The best ball striker golf had ever seen, Hogan described the sensation of hitting the perfect golf shot as a feeling that goes "up the shaft, right into your hands—and into your heart." His character is typified by his own quote: "I don't like the glamour. I just like the game."

Colin McLeod, secretary of the Carnoustie Golf Club, mentions that when visitors come to this hole, caddies warn: "Hogan's Alley is for the brave, but not for the faint hearted. One should favor the right of the center bunkers on this very difficult par five. Care must also be taken with your second shot as once again Jockey's Burn bites deeply into the right side of the fairway."

Hogan's courage may have persuaded Mr. McLeod to overlook the Hawk's acerbic humor. When asked for his impressions of the famed Carnoustie course upon his first and only visit, Hogan answered quickly: "I have a lawn mower back home in Texas . . . I'll send it over."

WATCHING THE SHOW AT AUGUSTA

Alvie Thompson was fascinated with the Ben Hogan swing he had learned from Marine Drive head professional Stan Leonard, and did everything he could to replicate the Magical Device. Alvie was hot on the trail of Hogan's secret as well. "I thought I had it a couple of times," he said, "but not quite." However, he did play well enough to win the Canadian Professional Golf Association title in 1962, earning him an invitation to the Masters at Augusta.

With this invitation—the dream of every young touring professional—Alvie hurried up Magnolia Way to the course early, to breathe in the atmosphere, and walk, and watch, and even play with golf's greats. He went with his Canuck pal George Knudson, winner of eight PGA tournaments with a tantalizing Masters second place finish in 1969 to the great putter George Archer. (Knudson was appraised by Jack Nicklaus as "a man with a million dollar swing and a ten cent putting stroke." Shagging balls on a few twilight evenings for Knudson at Point Grey, I found this to be true and had to bite my tongue when he picked the putter up so quickly at a sharp angle, only to decelerate back down to the ball). Alvie and George were very keen to watch Hogan close-up. But the administration of Augusta always arranged an isolated spot on the practice area so that the insular Ben Hogan could keep away from the microscopic eyes of the public as well as fellow players.

Nevertheless Alvie was determined, and led his two friends over a back fence through the pines not far from Ben Hogan, alone on the practice field hitting balls to his caddy.

Crouching behind bushes like a bunch of kids, they strained to dissect Hogan's swing secrets, when all of a sudden they saw Hogan wave to a security guard to beckon him over while pointing to the three golfers behind the bushes.

Well, everyone was terribly embarrassed to be paraded before the master himself and made to explain their behavior . . . but Hogan was understanding, after they had introduced themselves. He indicated a place where they could stand and got back to his practice.

Without a further word, Hogan hit balls for another hour while Alvie and his pals watched. Finally they excused themselves and left.

Hogan on the practice tee where observers could watch for swing details: Left hand in dorsiflexion gripping down on the handle, and the right knee rock-solid.

HELL HATH NO FURY . . .

It is tantalizing to compare super-athletes from different eras and to imagine them competing against each other—especially if you recognize that under the "performing arts" umbrella Ben Hogan and Tiger Woods are artists playing the most complex game in the world. I suspect that these two golfers, like athletes in the highest rankings of other fields such as Jesse Owens, Wayne Gretzky, Michael Jordan, and Babe Didrikson Zaharias, would have competed well in any era. How lucky some of us are to have seen them both.

It is also fascinating to compare the upbringing of Hogan and Tiger as children: Tiger with a solid, well structured two-parent family, and Hogan, who had precious little of that; Tiger with a disciplined former Green Beret as a manly model, and Hogan, whose father committed suicide in front of him at age nine.

Tiger went to Stanford with friends whom he could trust, and from whom he could learn. He was six foot one, 170 pounds, and had access to the latest

PHOTO CREDIT: Mike Lilly

Tiger Woods and his caddy at practice in happier times.

engineering triumphs to be applied to his equipment. "Bantam Ben" was a small man, who left school early trusting no one.

Tiger's determination appears to have risen naturally from an interaction with positive experiences and a resulting rising confidence. Hogan's determination, on the other hand, was likely developed within an atmosphere of quiet desperation.

It is a constant source of awe for me that two such superb competitors could have risen from such disparate beginnings, and yet both become so hungry for mastery of a game more complex than chess. Of course . . . isn't that one of the fascinations of golf for all of us?

From 1996 we watched Tiger's physique develop. The long lean and lanky boy named Eldrick, filled out to an impressive man-size 185 pounds capable of not just hitting the ball, but crushing it. We watched an amazing display of skilled shots. For example, at the 1999 Phoenix Open there was a truck-sized boulder dead-center of the fairway at 301 yards, and opponent Sergio Garcia of Spain hit straight down the middle only to come to rest against it. Tiger wound up his takeaway to full stretch and knocked a Ben Hogan power fade around the massive rock 340 yards into perfect position.

Tiger's short game too, was as remarkable as Hogan's and his presence created massive golf galleries who had never seen Hogan. Meanwhile, golf historians watched as Tiger mowed down sacred records: Arnold Palmer's seven major championships; Ben Hogan's nine majors (although he claimed ten for the Hale American Open championship during World War II) as he relentlessly pursued—without apology or malice—the Mount Everest of the major events, Jack Nicklaus with eighteen majors: six Masters, five PGA championships, four U.S. Opens, and three British Opens.

By the earlier age of thirty-four, Tiger had acquired four Masters, four PGA Championships, three U.S. Opens, and three British Opens. The race was on, with unbelievable escape shots like his 218 yard six iron in the 2000 Canadian Open at Glen Abbey in Ontario. With darkness closing in so that he could barely see the pin at the back corner of a crescent green curling around a black lake, Tiger looked at his wet lie in a rain-soaked fairway trap, sizing up whether he should play it safely to the fairway to his left in front of the green and settle for a long chip of 100 feet to the back corner in order to guarantee a par and a tie for the lead. A trap behind a fifteen-foot strip of green would snare the ball if long, and would demand a difficult following shot in the darkness back at the lake . . . what should he do? Well, he hunkered down, glared through the darkness at the postage stamp target and planted a six iron shot—that no one could see—twelve feet from the pin. Two putts and one birdie later, Tiger had won the Canadian Open title. Like Hogan, amazing.

And then one crazy day in the late autumn of 2009, just before Tiger's invitational tournament at Thousand Oaks, California, where the world's best golfers were invited by the host to display their skills in the treacherous and demanding forest where Errol Flynn had made the famous film *The Adventures of Robin Hood*, things changed. What happened next was the stuff that made Hollywood: fierce drama, heavy sex, and wicked betrayal.

On November 27, 2009, we awoke to the news release that Tiger had been in a car accident! Was he hurt? Was this another disaster . . . just as Hogan had suffered? How serious were the injuries? It appeared that it was no more than cuts and a mouthful of blood. His wife was seen bashing out the window of Tiger's Cadillac SUV with a golf club, apparently in a rescue attempt to get her husband out and to safety. He had just glanced off a fire hydrant while exiting his driveway at 2:15 in the morning and had careened into a neighbor's tree.

Wait a minute—2:15 AM? What's going on here?

Men in locker rooms exchanged knowing glances. They knew what life must be like on the "Great American Circus Trail," where alpha males travel from glen to glen—like Mustang stallions looking to sow wild oats. Wilt Chamberlain had told them. The seven-foot, three-hundred-pound basketball star for Philadelphia, scored a hundred points against the New York Knicks one night, and after retirement, let slip that his total conquests in the 'social arena' totaled more than twenty thousand groupies—all interested in basketball we suppose. Magic Johnson, point guard for Los Angeles Lakers, had confirmed the extent of post game antics with the background story of his HIV problem. Women waited for these prime physical specimens who came to town now and then, to play their games—basketball, baseball, football, hockey—it didn't matter which. These warrior risk-takers, flushed with the juices of life, were well paid, with plenty of money to entertain women looking for anonymous fun. And best of all, thought the ladies, they were scheduled to leave town the next day—so no boyfriend, no pastor, no rabbi would be any wiser about cheap thrills. "A fabulous fling . . . just one of those things."

Lots of men heard the titillating tales about golf. There would be a smiling reference to superstars whose caddies carried a spare key to their loop's hotel room. After making the cut, a golfer might think of the pressure-filled demands of weekend play following days of practice, focus, and stress. A flirtatious smile might encourage the golfer to nudge his caddy with a nod toward "the lady with the expensive sun-glasses."

"This is the pro's hotel room key—want it?" The lady had two choices: yes or no. The odds were good that someone would take it. And the rumor was, that it is twice as bad on the LPGA circuit, where heterosexual members of the gallery likened the electric atmosphere to "swimming in shark-infested waters" as some in those galleries flashed their own brand of flirtatious smiles.

Locker rooms were soon crowded with jokes: "What do baby seals and Tiger Woods have in common? Well, both could wind up getting clubbed by a Norwegian." There would be chuckles and grins, but no guffaws—it was not that type of atmosphere. These witticisms were *entré nous* exchanges from men who assumed that, more than likely, most there had skeletons to keep in the closet. They knew that periodically males have very real physiological pressures which demanded some sort of relief, which may not be, at times, all that convenient to social mores. And they certainly knew that men really were from Mars, and were just as convinced that women were from Venus. Many observers knew—for sure—that women might overlook a temporary this or that . . . but public embarrassment was not on the list.

The media were restrained at first—even polite—as they had been while following Tiger's rich and illustrious pathway to the rank of most recognizable, most inspirational, most successful, and most sought-after athlete on this planet. In October 2009 he was invited to the Shanghai Open Championships to make certain that China's golf industry would benefit from the play of quite possibly the best golfer the world has ever seen . . . he was paid a reported $3 million appearance money. Tiger fulfilled all hopes—and won—then boarded his private jet for the Australian Masters in Melbourne at the Kingston Heath course. Australia had not seen Tiger in the flesh for a while, and wanted him badly, believing that golf in Oz needed a publicity boost—and so they ponied up another $3 million for appearance money. Yes, he won with a special flash of talent shooting a tidy sixty-eight in front of appreciative record crowds for another pot of 270,000 Australian dollars.

Randy old Sam Snead, who made no more than $2,000 for any of his eighty-two PGA tournament wins, would be smacking his lips with tales of Tiger's lifestyle. Ben Hogan, after his early years of scratching for $75 or $100, would have shaken his head in disbelief at the level of today's prize money that he had helped elevate to unbelievable levels. When Tiger turned pro in 1996 it was $66 million; by 2009 the total amount up for grabs was $279 million. Even PGA card carrying players of the lowest ranking were helped along by Monday pro-ams with guaranteed appearance money of $3,000 with further gains to be made on the Wednesday pro-am—just in case they didn't make the cut for weekend play where the "real money" was. In 2009, no fewer than ninety-one PGA touring pros won more than $1 million in official prize money. I wonder if they ever think of how much direct influence Hogan and Palmer and Tiger had upon the build-up of that bonanza?

Ben Hogan would have glowered sternly at the hint of any impropriety that Tiger might have committed. Never has there been even a rumor of scandal attached to Hogan's name—not a hint.

It will be interesting to note the effect, if any, that Tiger's moral dilemma will have on his game. Will embarrassment spoil the aloof concentration drilled into him by his father? Will catcalls and boobirds intrude on his focus for the moment? It was noticed that few players were interviewed during what was once an exaggerated cliché but which could now truly could be called a "media frenzy." Sweden's Jesper Parnevik, who once introduced his family nanny to Tiger, was quick to conclusions, and quick to side with a fellow Scandinavian by stating that he was "sorry that he introduced her to such a philanderer."

Ben Crane, a PGA player who had finished the 2009 season with earnings of $1.7 million putting him in fifty-first place on the Money Leaders List, was quoted as being very critical of Tiger and his infidelities—which soon numbered more than a dozen young women (mostly cocktail waitresses) who blushingly admitted to affairs ranging from "exciting" to "torrid." After one week, Crane and Charles Warren denied the statements attributed to them and threatened a lawsuit to the tabloid in question. Jack Nicklaus, the old master, was questioned. Very seriously, and very thoughtfully, he looked at the reporter. "Time usually heals all wounds. I think the hardest pressure is obviously his family. That's a private matter for him and his family . . . . Tiger is a great athlete and will no doubt solve his problems on his own."

What will Tiger's reaction to his critics be? A review of his father's training might give us a clue. Ben Hogan had a tough beginning in a desperately poor economic period—the Dirty Thirties, the worst in modern history—and yet he claimed that deprivation made him stronger. And when Hogan was knocked off the top spot as the best golfer in the world because of his devastating car crash, he rose again by the sheer power of hard work, and because of a few small changes, was better than ever. He said, "When I get up in the morning, I can't wait to get to the course and hit balls."

Tiger's father told him, "There will never be an opponent who will outwork you." There is no reason not to conclude that Tiger believed him then, and believes him now. There is the likelihood that Tiger will be terribly embarrassed for a time, but that embarrassment will surely turn to anger, and from there to determination, when he realizes what he has lost, and who his real friends were . . . or were not.

Hogan's father left him to fight his way alone. If Tiger develops the same feelings of rejection, he could react in exactly the same way as Hogan with this new isolation: I'll show those bastards . . . I'll show them all.

Ben Hogan had searing focus and neurotic determination. Tiger could be the same—no more Mr. Nice Guy!

(This was written December 2009 while wondering how it will all turn out.)

By April the Masters at Augusta announced that Tiger would end his exile after months of soul-searching, soul-baring therapy. The chastised champion apologized publicly and hoped he might, some day, be forgiven.

With an ovation greeting his first drive at Augusta from tee box number one, golf fans let him know that they had accepted his public flagellation and welcomed him back to the game.

All were silently hoping that his was a marriage that could be saved. And this wish was ironically brought out with great force as Phil Mickelson stroked in his birdie putt on the final hole for his third green jacket. He quickly shook hands with his opponent Lee Westwood, next the caddies, then hurried into the gallery where his family waited. He collapsed into the arms of his wife who was smiling, though weak from chemotherapy and the emotion of the day. Mickelson held his partner in a bear hug as if he would never let her go. They cried together and held each other for an age before he acknowledged the rest of his group. But he never let go of his wife's hand . . . so precious was the moment.

FROM ONE MASTER ABOUT ANOTHER:

Ben Crenshaw, the golf historian who won Masters Championships in 1984 and 1995, had much high praise for Hogan's putting technique during a flight from Pebble Beach to San Francisco after the Crosby Pro-Am. He explained the details of Hogan's putting stroke to Andy Williams of "Moon River" fame who was hanging on every image. Crenshaw also said this of Hogan in *I Remember Ben Hogan* by Michael J. Towle:

"Although Hogan will always be remembered as arguably the finest ball-striker ever, in my opinion his quick, analytical mind was probably his strongest personality trait as a champion golfer. He was a bit of a loner and was actually somewhat shy, but he found a great passion and love for the solitude of golf and its unique challenge."

Ben Hogan's balance and grace at practice—his lifelong love.

PHOTO CREDIT: Ross Collver

SKIN OF SUN DRIED LEATHER

Dick Zokol, the Canadian Amateur Champion in 1981, went to Brigham Young University on a full scholarship, where he roomed with Lanny Wadkins. After captaining the university team to NCAA victory he turned professional, winning five titles and twenty top ten finishes.

Zokol came onto the radar screen with a second place finish at the Hawaiian Open in 1981. The runner-up prize was made all the sweeter by an invitation from the past winners of the Colonial Open to join them and Ben Hogan for dinner as "The Champion's Choice" in recognition of a new talent on the scene.

The dinner with Hogan—the man whom no one could understand—was a special treat, but Hogan's enigmatic style was exemplified when Byron Nelson, Hogan's caddy friend, fellow competitor, and sometimes two-ball partner, was called on to speak. In recognition of Nelson's marvelous career where, at the beginning, he beat Hogan out of many prizes, many times, the audience stood as one to applaud "Lord Byron" as he walked to the podium.

Only Hogan remained seated.

A SOFTER SIDE

Hogan loved his wife, Valerie, but showed the rest of the world a thick skin. Even close associates and business partners knew that he held his emotions—which included the gift of friendship—under a tight rein.

As the caddies and close golfing colleagues experienced: If Hogan liked you, he would do anything for you. But there was always an emotional distance between the acquaintance and the shy man whose boyhood was damaged beyond repair.

However, there was one who, to everyone's surprise, gained a spot in Hogan's life like few others could. Max was a stray dog who hung around Shady Oaks, and before long, he took to following Hogan to his morning practice session where he would watch dutifully as "the Hawk" indulged in his life-long routine. After a time, Hogan arranged for the club to care for the dog and to look after its food supply.

When Max died, members were shocked to see the usually completely controlled Hogan fall to his knees sobbing.

HOGAN'S LAST SHOT

The following revelation by Mike Wright, now director of golf at Shady Oaks in Texas, is my favorite Ben Hogan story because it shows what happens when you ingrain Mr. Hogan's swing system. I found that if I'm late for a tee time and don't have time for a bucket of warm-up balls, there's no need to panic. A slow, stretching swing with two clubs—as Hogan did—while mentally reviewing your key points is sufficient. So help me . . . . the waggle brings the left hand timing back into focus, and gives you enough memory for a decent first shot. What amazed me was that it also works on the green for your first putt of the day—simply rehearse the putt with your mirror drill—nothing moves but the Magical Device. Hogan knew what he was doing—and so will you.

Even if we review all of Mr. Hogan's sixty-three PGA Tour trophies and his domination of "ten" majors that leaves us in breathless admiration for the beauty of his shot—like the one iron at Merion in 1950 to win the U.S. Open—there remains one more story that demands your attention. It was related to me by Mike Wright, when as a young professional at Shady Oaks in Westworth Village. He was, very likely, the last person to see Ben Hogan strike a ball.

Hogan had said, "Once you have developed a good golf swing and acquired the knowledge of how to make the most of it, nobody can take it away from you."

However, as advancing age overtook the great champion to the point where even his practicing dwindled away, it was doubted that he still had the ability to return a controlled clubface with power to the ball as he had done for so many years. He must have wondered that himself because unexpectedly, when closing in on eighty years, he came to the pro shop late one afternoon and asked the pro for his driver and three balls.

Mike obliged and watched from the shop window as the Hawk went out to the tenth tee and plugged one in. The hole was 370 yards and well trapped. To open the green to the best angle for a tucked left pin, the drive should be to be right of center and past the fairway traps. Mr. Hogan hit three balls with his signature power fade. He smiled and nodded as they all came to rest beside each other in the perfect spot.

Mr. Hogan then returned to the shop where he handed in his club, thanked the pro with a satisfied wave of the hand, then left the game forever, passing away in 1997 at the age of eighty-five.

PHOTO CREDIT: Kevin Coughlin

Relaxed, confident, and debonair, Hogan caught in repose by artist Kevin Coughlin, his hands still in the mold that made him the best of the best.

ACKNOWLEDGEMENTS

Writing a golf book as an amateur takes a lot of chutzpah (some would say shameless impudence) and a demand for more work than ever anticipated—especially concerning the photographs and artwork. So I would like to thank some key people for their help in the completion of this look back on Ben Hogan.

Helen Hunt, my chief organizer, who was completely forgotten in the last book.

Sean Connery, with his Hogan spirit and timely encouragement.

Dr. Des Dwyer, who not only kept my injury-ridden body intact, but gave his time and knowledge of golf to early rough-draft editing.

Charles Hillman, with his unwavering enthusiasm for analyzing the details of this elusive game.

Dr. Marty Mclouglin, whose inquiring mind and myriad questions gave momentum to the difficult task of explaining the function of a golf swing's many moving parts.

My thanks to several golf professionals for their valuable advice: CJ Wilson, Jack Westover, Joe Jeroski, Wayne Hong, Drew Scollon, as well as PGA tour players Alvie Thompson and Dick Zokol.

Special thanks to Jeff Buder who, as Point Grey's head professional, provided me with several Hogan insights, and modeled the short game wherein he specializes—as when demonstrating his skills in the Canadian PGA Club Professional Championship in Florida in November 2009, finishing in a tie for first place.

Other models included: Yuya Kihara, Point Grey's Junior Champion; Professional Wayne Hong; Rose-Mary Basham, a Hogan-swing look-alike; and keen golfers James Boyle, Marty Mcloughlin, Des Dwyer, Paul Brown, Morgan Good, Ryan Cook, and Tasha Samuels visiting from the faraway Queen Charlotte Islands, now named Haida Gwaii—Islands of the Haida.

Photographers include Peter Burnet, Shelley Winfield, Stefan Winfield, and Mike Lilly, who has steered three sons into very good golf. And thanks to Tim Mah for demonstrating the similar demands of fitness and balance for dance and golf.

There were three artists whose paintings helped illustrate this book, necessary because new Hogan photographs are difficult to find, and most tend to be shots of the swing-finish rather than photos which show specific key points of the master's technique. Bill McLuckie painted the Hogan chapter images. Ken West provided some lively paintings and diagrams. And many thanks to Kyle Cormier for introducing me to Kevin Coughlin, the artist from Winnipeg, who allowed us to use his Texas Golf Greats image as a last glimpse of Ben Hogan in repose. His other Texas Greats paintings were of Hogan's formidable rival and caddy friend, Byron Nelson, then Ben Crenshaw, who taught me a lot about putting, and Tom Kite who introduced me to the value of properly fitted club shafts.

My appreciation to Colette Miller in the administration office at Point Grey who was always very helpful and considerate, as was General Manager Brad Pinnell.

Thanks also to Mitch Woolrich for his business advice. To Abigail Gehring for her coordination of 231 images with captions; not an easy task. And thanks to Mark Weinstein, the Senior Editor at Skyhorse Publishing who was so helpful and patient concerning the thousands of problems involved with this golf book—his tenth edit.

SELECTED BIBLIOGRAPHY

Books:

Andrisani, John. *The Hogan Way*. New York: Harper Collins, 2004.

Bertrand, Tom, and Printer Bowler. *The Secret of Hogan's Swing*. Hoboken: John Wiley & Sons, Inc., 2006.

Davis, Martin. *Ben Hogan: The Man Behind the Mystique*. Greenwich: American Golfer, 2002.

Dodson, James. *Ben Hogan: An American Life*. New York: Doubleday, 2004.

Farnsworth, Craig. *See It & Sink It*. New York: HarperCollins, 1997.

Frost, Mark. *The Match*. New York: Hyperion Books, 2007.

"Golf." *New York Times Encyclopedia of Sports*. Volume 5. New York: Arno Press, 1979.

Hardy, Jim, and John Andrisani. *The Plane Truth for Golfers*. New York: McGraw-Hill, 2005.

Hogan, Ben. *Ben Hogan's Five Lessons: The Modern Fundamentals of Golf*. New York: Simon and Schuster, 1957.

Hogan, Ben. *Power Golf*. New York: A.S. Barnes, 1948.

Leadbetter, David, with Lorne Rubenstein. *The Fundamentals of Hogan*. New York: Doubleday, 2000.

Lohren, Carl, with Al Barkow. *Getting Set for Golf*. New York: Viking, 1995.
McLean, Jim. *The Eight Step Swing*. New York: HarperCollins, 2001.
Middlecopp, Cary. *The Golf Swing*. Springfield, NJ: Burford Books, 1974.
Minni, Scott. *Smash and Carve Golf: The Art of Ball Striking*. New York: Smash and Carve Golf, 1999.
Morrison, Ian. *Great Moments In Golf*. London: Bison Books, 1987.
Nicklaus, Jack. *Golf My Way*. New York: Simon & Schuster, 2002.
Palmer, Arnold. *The Arnold Palmer Method*. New York: Dell Publishing, 1967.
Palmer, Arnold, and James Dobson. *A Golfer's Life*. New York: Ballantine Books, 1999.
Sampson, Curt. *Hogan*. New York: Broadway Books, 1997.
Sinnette, Calvin. *Forbidden Fairways*. Chelsea: Sleeping Bear Press, 1998.
Skyzinski, Rich. *The Quotable Hogan*. Nashville: TowleHouse, 2001.
Snead, Sam. *How to Play Golf*. New York: Garden City Publishing, 1946.
Thomas, Bob. *Ben Hogan's Secret*. New York: MacMillan Publishing Company, 1997.
Towle, Michael. *I Remember Ben Hogan*. Nashville: Cumberland House, 2000.
Vasquez, Jody. *Afternoons with Mr. Hogan*. New York: Gotham Books, 2005.
Woods, Tiger. *How I Play Golf*. New York: Warner Books, 2001.
Magazines:
Failure magazine. July. 2002. "The Greatest Golfer the World Has Never Known."
Golf April 1978.
Golf Digest April 8, 1955.
Golf Digest March 1994.
Golf Digest August 2004
GolfStyle Summer 2007.
Impact magazine July 2009. "Planks and Bridges: An anti-Rotation Abdominal Workout."
Life magazine August 8, 1955.
Ode magazine October 2008.

INDEX